Administering Justice

Administering Justice

Placing the Chief Justice
in American State Politics

RICHARD L. VINING JR.
TEENA WILHELM

University of Michigan Press
Ann Arbor

Published in the United States of America by the
University of Michigan Press
Manufactured in the United States of America
Printed on acid-free paper
First published August 2023

A CIP catalog record for this book is available from the British Library.

Library of Congress Control Number: 2023013022
LC record available at https://lccn.loc.gov/2023013022

ISBN 978-0-472-07630-7 (hardcover : alk. paper)
ISBN 978-0-472-05630-9 (paper : alk. paper)
ISBN 978-0-472-90369-6 (open access ebook)

DOI: https://doi.org/10.3998/mpub.12079561

The University of Michigan Press's open access publishing program is made possible thanks to additional funding from the University of Michigan Office of the Provost and the generous support of contributing libraries.

Cover photograph: View of the atrium, Nathan Deal Judicial Center, Atlanta, Georgia. Photograph by Saskia E. Houghton, reproduced by permission.

To my parents, Rick and Rosemary

—R.V.

To Matt, who helps me see it through

—T.W.

Contents

Digital materials related to this title can be found on
the Fulcrum platform via the following citable URL:
https://doi.org/10.3998/mpub.12079561

Tables

Figures

Acknowledgments

We would not have been able to complete this project—our first book—without help. We are indebted to colleagues, graduate students, and other professionals whose contributions were meaningful for this finished product.

Much of the material in this book was inspired by an interest in chief justices that began early in our careers at the University of Georgia. Over the last decade, both graduate and undergraduate students (some of whom have become our colleagues and collaborators) helped with data collection. Our appreciation goes to Emily Wanless, David Hughes, Ethan Boldt, Bryan Black, Alyson Hendricks, Austin Petrie, Mariliz Kastberg-Leonard, Taylor Wilhelm, and Matthew Holmquist.

We work with a group of genuinely lovely human beings at the University of Georgia, and credit goes to our colleagues for a truly supportive work environment. Jamie Carson has been a helpful guide in the publication process. More generally, his office is a place of problem solving and advice giving. Conversations with Christy Boyd helped our understanding and measurement of judicial diversity. Michael Lynch, Joe Ornstein, and Garrett Vande Kamp willingly assisted us with methodological and software questions. Finally, the guidance of our wise colleagues and mentors Susan Haire and John Maltese has shaped this and all our projects.

Court personnel were also important for this project. These included various state supreme court librarians, historians, and public information officers who answered our emails and phone calls and aided our efforts

xiv · Acknowledgments

to track down archival documents likely never before requested. Their work provided information we could not obtain otherwise, especially during a worldwide pandemic. Our gratitude also extends to the nameless record keepers managing state supreme court websites, who have no idea how much academic research they inform. We are extremely grateful for the work done by the National Center for State Courts. Senior analyst William (Bill) Raftery has long been a valuable NCSC resource for us, and data collected and shared by NCSC research associate Allison Trochesset (who also helped us during her time as a graduate student) was important as well.

Finally, we are grateful to the states' chief justices for serving as such a compelling subject. We are honored to get to share what we know about them with the rest of the world.

Introduction

For observers of American politics, former Alabama chief justice Roy S. Moore is synonymous with controversy and political spectacle. Moore fed the Alabama news cycle for nearly two decades after hanging a wooden plaque of the Ten Commandments in his Etowah County courtroom in 1999. He entered statewide politics in 2000 as a candidate for chief justice of the Alabama Supreme Court, a position he won despite opposition from establishment Republicans and a Democratic rival. Shortly after he became the court's leader in 2001, he used his authority to install a granite monument of the Ten Commandments in the rotunda of the Alabama Judicial Building. In 2003, Chief Justice Moore refused to obey the federal district court ruling that ordered the removal of this monument. The resulting standoff sparked public rallies attended by thousands of supporters and led by noteworthy speakers that included Moore, Jerry Falwell, and prominent conservative activists. Ultimately, Moore was found to have violated the Alabama Canons of Judicial Ethics and was removed from the bench (Clark 2005).

When Moore was elected chief justice a second time several years later, he continued to engage in provocative behavior. While running for election in 2012, he argued that legalizing same-sex marriage would lead to the "ultimate destruction of our country" (Chandler 2016). In January 2015, during Moore's second term as chief justice, U.S. district judge Callie V. Granade of the Southern District of Alabama declared the state's same-sex marriage ban to be unconstitutional. Chief Justice Moore responded defiantly, arguing that federal court judges lacked the authority to overturn Alabama's Sanctity of Marriage Amendment and that the state's judges remained bound by it. After the 2015 ruling in *Obergefell v. Hodges* (576 U.S. 644), in which the U.S. Supreme Court recognized same-sex marriage as protected by the Constitution, Moore unilaterally issued an administrative order declaring that his state's probate judges had "a ministerial duty not to issue any marriage licenses" to same-sex couples (Jonsson 2016). He argued that the Supreme Court's ruling, based on a case from another federal circuit, did not apply to Alabama.

Moore's defiance of the Supreme Court ultimately led to ethics complaints and to his second removal from the Alabama bench, in September 2016. Moore responded bitterly to his dismissal, calling it the product of a "politically motivated effort" undertaken by "radical homosexual and transgender groups" because he was opposed to their "immoral agenda" (Chandler 2017). Interestingly, Moore's two removals from public office did not deter his interest in Alabama politics. He ran unsuccessfully for governor in 2006 and 2010 and for U.S. Senate in 2017 and 2020.[1]

Roy Moore's tenure as chief justice and the willingness of Alabama voters to reinstate him underscore several significant points about judicial leaders. First, administrative powers set chief justices apart from their colleagues and have meaningful consequences. After all, the actions that brought Chief Justice Moore to national prominence were primarily related to administrative leadership of the state judiciary rather than to intracourt leadership or case outcomes. Second, politics and the judiciary are not mutually exclusive. While courts are sometimes depicted as existing outside the political realm, Moore's tenure tells us that this is not accurate. In fact, these events illustrate that the chief justice can reflect the tenor of a state political environment. Although Moore's actions were controversial, his appeal to Alabama voters was affirmed by reelection in 2012.

Roy Moore's time as the leader of the Alabama high court demonstrates how a chief justice can be a consequential actor in the state political environment without casting a vote or writing a judicial opinion. Moore used his capacity as leader of the judiciary to issue a sweeping administrative order with clear policy implications. He also interacted with state political elites, media, and the public to draw attention to his desired policy goals. Such interactions exist outside a chief justice's formal role in case adjudication. The extrajudicial responsibilities of state chief justices allow them to influence reform of the justice system, the comity of interbranch relations, and public perceptions of legal issues.

They may even allow a chief justice to affect political issues within the state that are not exclusively related to courts and judges.

Chief justices have a variety of formal and informal powers that give them a significant role in state politics. These responsibilities are beyond the scope of their intracourt duties, making them vital leaders for their states' courts as well as key participants in state governments. The powers and responsibilities of the state chief justices differ, as do the institutional designs of their offices and the political conditions within states. There is also ample variation in the kinds of individuals who serve as state chief justices and in the spheres of influence they occupy. State supreme courts are seldom led by a bombastic individual like Roy Moore, and not every state supreme court is structured in a way that would facilitate the selection of a similar leader.

Few chief justices make national headlines like Moore. Perhaps consequently, political scientists seldom study the leaders of state courts. We thus have a limited understanding of the diverse group of individuals leading state high courts and of the institutional structures in which they serve. Moreover, little attention is given to the less visible work chief justices do when leading their court systems.

In this book, we analyze the often-overlooked role of chief justices as leaders of the judicial branch. We are motivated by this question: What is the role of the chief justice in the state political environment? A survey of extant research reveals that our understanding of this role is incomplete because there is little collective information about state chief justices and because existing studies focus narrowly on intracourt leadership. That focus overlooks key responsibilities of modern chief justices. Consequently, we build our research strategy for this book on the fundamental premise that state chief justices are of consequence because of what they do both within and outside their courts. We believe the traditional narrative about judicial leadership does not account for the full influence of state court leaders.

State Supreme Courts and Their Leaders

Although public interest is more often focused on the U.S. Supreme Court, state high courts are key venues for the disposition of legal matters. American courts are organized into a dual system, with federal and state courts operating in distinct jurisdictions. The vast majority of judicial activity in the United States, about 95 percent of all case dispositions, happens at the state level.[2] State court systems are organized similar to the federal courts, with trial courts at the bottom and high courts at the top. Most states, though not all, have an intermediate appellate court for the initial round of appeals. The highest courts in the states are charged with the interpretation of state constitutions and the practice of judicial review. These courts processed more than 71,000 cases in 2018.[3] While it is feasible for cases to originate in state courts and reach the docket of the U.S. Supreme Court, it is exceedingly rare relative to the population of cases within state jurisdictions. For a state court case to reach the U.S. Supreme Court, it must concern federal law, treaties, or the Constitution and meet a set of conditions that invoke a federal question during the state proceedings (Perry 1991, 302–3). In addition, the federal justices must select it for their discretionary docket. In recent terms, the Supreme Court has decided less than 100 cases (often only 70–80) from the pool of roughly 8,000 cases appealed to them from inferior courts. Not surprisingly, most state supreme court rulings do not receive additional review. These decisions are the final say on consequential legal matters.

Litigants rely on state courts to resolve state constitutional issues that do not have a federal equivalent (Emmert and Traut 1992). State constitutions tend to be much longer and more detailed than the federal Constitution, addressing matters of policy and governance delegated to the states (Kincaid 1988). The average length of a state constitution in 2019 was approximately 39,000 words, while the federal Constitution is just under 8,000 words.[4] In addition to addressing state constitutional issues, state and local governments pass laws and regulations relevant to their constituencies that are unlikely to be addressed by the federal government. As a result, ample opportunities exist for state high courts to have the last word on issues, given the minimal likelihood that federal courts will intervene.

The relative autonomy of state supreme courts in the dual U.S. court system was both a cause and a consequence of the new judicial federalism in the 1970s (Brennan 1977). That movement urged litigants and jurists to rely on state constitutions and state courts to resolve novel legal disputes and to establish rights and protections beyond those developed by federal law. It established a legally recognized "methodology," sanctioned by state and federal courts, for keeping issues on state court dockets and preventing intrusion by federal courts. The movement was swift, as state courts asserted substantial independence by the 1980s (Collins and Galie 1986; Emmert and Traut 1992). Substantively, state high courts took the lead in such important issue areas as gay rights (Nemacheck 2017; Zschirnt 2016), criminal procedure, education finance, privacy (Cauthen 1999), and zoning (Tarr 1997).

The 52 courts of last resort in the American states (Texas and Oklahoma both have separate high courts for civil and criminal cases) operate within diverse sets of political and institutional conditions. The institutional variation among state supreme courts allows scholars to examine them from a comparative perspective. Because the state supreme courts differ from each other, we can assess the impact of institutional design and judges' characteristics in ways not feasible in research on federal courts. The institutional differences include size, method of selection and/or retention, and length of terms and tenure. Institutional design can vary across and within states over time (Kritzer 2020; Marcin 2015). Shifts in the design of state judicial systems have happened both in waves and at idiosyncratic moments.

State supreme courts also feature much more variation among their members than is found on the U.S. Supreme Court. The judges of the state supreme courts are diverse in terms of professional experience, legal training, gender, and racial backgrounds. U.S. Supreme Court justices have mostly been white males, with other demographic groups joining the court in small numbers since the 1960s. Only 17 individuals have served as Chief Justice of the United States, and in the past 50 years, that office has been occupied by just three men: Warren E. Burger (1969–86), William H. Rehnquist (1986–2005), and John G. Roberts Jr. (2005 to present). All three were appointed by conservative Republican presidents and shared similar judicial philosophies. All were confirmed by the U.S. Senate for terms "during good behavior" (i.e., life tenure) and faced neither reelection nor reappointment. The stability of that office limits scholarly ability to analyze the impact of variation on court leadership. In contrast, diversity exists among states' chief justices in ways absent on the U.S. Supreme Court, with variation in the characteristics of state court leaders, in the methods of their selection and retention, and in their powers and roles. That variation invites scholarly analysis of the responsibilities, priorities, and effectiveness of state court leaders.

Facets of Judicial Leadership

Social scientists have studied chief justices for more than half a century, with the primary focus being leadership within courts (e.g., Cross and Lindquist 2006; Danelski 1960; Gray and Miller 2021; M.E.K. Hall and Windett 2016; Haynie 1992; Walker, Epstein, and Dixon 1988). Specifically, scholars have focused on a chief justice's impact on either case outcomes or the judicial decision-making process. As a point of distinction, our research in this book is not fixed on those facets of judicial leadership. Instead, we focus on the administrative and political duties that take up a chief justice's remaining time and effort. These obligations are a substantial component of a chief justice's responsibilities.

The most influential explanation of chief justice leadership comes from a paper prepared by David J. Danelski for the 1960 meeting of the American Political Science Association. He argued that federal chief justices can engage in task leadership and social leadership. Task leadership revolves around the technical aspects of the Supreme Court's decision process. It involves presenting case information, leading discussion, pointing out agreement and disagreement, and calling votes. Social leadership is focused "on keeping the Court socially cohesive" (Danelski 1960, 1). It involves efforts to relieve tension during the Court's conference discussions by fostering dialogue, inviting compromise, and cutting off debate. Social leadership smooths out the rough corners of the human side of deliberation.[5]

The theoretical foundation provided by Danelski influenced studies of both federal and state chief justices. Scholars mostly oriented that research toward case processing and the degree to which chief justices could "marshal" their courts (Murphy 1964). Related research informs much of our understanding of the leadership abilities of the chief justice in case selection, oral argument, decision-making, coalition formation, consensus building, opinion assignment, and opinion writing. Scholars have concluded that a chief justice's influence within a court, whether at the federal or state level, depends on the institutional design of the office (Gray and Miller 2021; M.E.K. Hall and Windett 2016) as well as the ideological proclivities and personal style of the individual who occupies the position (e.g., Walker, Epstein, and Dixon 1988).

The line of inquiry that examines judicial leadership typically does not address the administrative and political activities on which state chief justices spend a substantial portion of their time, central duties for many modern state court leaders (Raftery 2017; Shepard 2009a, 2009b). Consider, for example, remarks by former South Dakota governor Dennis M. Daugaard about former chief justice David E. Gilbertson:

> Unlike some other supreme court justices around the nation, our Supreme Court Chief Justice cared about policymaking. He cared about our criminal justice system and he was very active in the reform

of our adult and juvenile systems. He had many policy initiatives of his own that make him stand out among his peers. I think about him as the driver on the bus. And he always put a bunch of people in the seats with him when he dedicated himself to a program. He had a lot of credibility with the legislature and the Governor's Office. (Ewald 2022)

Daugaard's comments suggest that Gilbertson's direction of much of his effort toward the policy arena was viewed positively by other political elites in South Dakota.

Administrative responsibilities frequently demand time and attention that chief justices would otherwise spend on the traditional duties of judges (Smith and Feldman 2001). This demand is not widely acknowledged and is sometimes overlooked by observers and critics of chief justices. For example, when Robert F. Stephens of Kentucky ran for reelection as chief justice in 1984, the campaign rhetoric of his challenger, Lexington attorney Julian R. Gabbard, denigrated the chief justice's work ethic, citing that Stephens authored very few opinions on the high court. In response to the challenger's criticism, Stephens explained that he took part in most of the court's cases, but that the duties of his office were primarily devoted to court administration. Stephens estimated that he spent 75 percent of his time on administrative work, "from preparing a budget to testifying before the legislature." Stephens won the election handily (Hackett 1984).

The most fundamental source of a chief justice's extrajudicial responsibilities is the role as head of the state judicial branch. Minnesota Chief Justice Eric J. Magnuson identified himself as "the head of a 3,000-person judicial branch led by a single policy-making body, the Judicial Council, which I chair." He further elaborated, "The duties of the chief justice go far beyond deciding cases; they encompass significant administrative responsibilities touching the whole range of Court functioning" (Magnuson 2008). That a single individual can lead and influence the whole range of court functions within a state is significant given that most citizens will interact with a state's justice system in some way. Lloyd A. Karmeier, chief justice of the Illinois Supreme Court, explained,

In one way or another, the judicial branch impacts all Illinois residents on a daily basis. The more highly visible examples are litigants or witnesses involved in civil actions, or prosecutors and defense counsel in criminal cases. These are the stuff of television and movies. But even those many individuals who have never even entered a courthouse are touched by the justice system on a regular basis in more mundane ways—as jurors, perhaps, or through remote payment of citations, fines or fees, or simply as residents of a community that benefit from judicial decisions and the justice stakeholders working to ensure the effective and efficient operation of the legal system. (Karmeier 2018)

The chief justice is legally responsible for administration of the state judiciary in all 50 states, either alone (in 31 states), as leader of the state high court (in 17 states), or as head of the judicial council (in 2 states).[6] Even in states where sole authority does not lie with the chief justice, the high court's leader traditionally appoints and oversees the state court administrator who has operational and functional authority over the state judiciary (Turner and Breslin 2006).

Alongside the purely administrative facets of chief justice leadership, responsibilities also flow from the political role of the position. As the most visible representative of the judiciary, the chief justice is the leading advocate for judicial reforms. Court leaders help to establish the legislative agenda for court reform through formal channels, including the judicial council or the State of the Judiciary report, and through informal channels, such as relationships with political elites. Court leaders may also influence the success of the agenda (Wilhelm, Vining, Boldt, and Black 2020). As the preceding discussions of Roy Moore and David Gilbertson illustrate, a chief justice can garner public attention and the prestige and profile associated with the position can be utilized to highlight policy exigencies if a chief justice is so inclined.

A chief justice can also have a direct influence on policymaking for the courts. The chief who anticipates the impact that legislation will have on the judiciary before it becomes law can use the weight of the chief justice position to wield influence. For an indication of how often this happens in the state political environment, consider reflections by Ellen A. Peters, chief justice of the Connecticut Supreme Court, as described by Harvard law professor David J. Barron.

Wholly apart from its resolution of cases in court, state judicial administrators, [Peters] concludes, are busy monitoring legislation as it wends its way to the floor—all the while seeking to influence the pending bills so as to avoid future points of conflict. The precise bounds of the type of legislation that triggers interest and thus influence is nowhere specified clearly. (Barron 2008, 30)

As anecdotes throughout this book confirm, these observations by Chief Justice Peters are not unusual. Court leaders tend to be politically engaged in the state policymaking environment with clear goals in mind. The degree to which chief justices embrace this facet of judicial leadership will vary. Some chief justices are comfortable with press conferences and politically charged headlines, while others prefer to be less aggressive in their leadership style. The time horizon for reform efforts also differs among court leaders because they may be either short-term or long-term chiefs (Shepard 2009a). Regardless of how they differ, chief justices frequently operate within the political environment as more than participants in adjudication. In this book, we give these activities the scholarly attention they deserve.

Placing the Chief Justices in State Politics: An Overview

We consider chief justices outside their court-focused leadership that is usually referenced, focusing instead on how court leaders fit within the state political environment. We advance our inquiry in two parts. In chapters 1–2, we provide a necessary baseline of information about court leadership positions and the individuals who serve in them. In chapters 3–5, we focus on different facets of chief justice leadership in the state political environment: administration, advocacy, and political engagement.

While much is known about the U.S. Supreme Court's chief justices (from, e.g., Danelski and Ward 2016), the same cannot be said for chief justice positions across the states. Given that absence of knowledge, the first part of our research provides a foundational analysis. In chapter 1, we examine the structure of the chief justice position across the states. We provide insight about the variations in how chief justices are selected to lead the courts and in how long they remain there. We also examine the extent to which selection methods can influence the kinds of chief justices that are selected, with a specific focus on ideology. Chapter 2 examines individuals who occupy the office. We give particular attention to diversity among those who have served as chief justice, including how that diversity is influenced by judicial selection methods.

In the second part of our research, we give substantial attention to chief justice leadership outside the court. In chapter 3, we explore the formal and informal administrative responsibilities of chief justices. We trace the historical movement toward centralization of judicial administration in the states, highlighting the importance of chief justices in these endeavors. We also explore the leadership of modern chief justices in judicial reform efforts.

In chapter 4, we focus on chief justice advocacy efforts for the state judiciary. Our narrative highlights the necessity of this leadership for maintenance of state courts, recognizing how it can often be a magnet for (wanted or unwanted) political attention and court curbing by the other branches of government. We pay specific attention to the chief justice's agenda-setting responsibilities and provide broad analysis of State of the Judiciary addresses over time. Chapter 4 reveals much about the types of judicial reform policies requested by chief justices and about what factors influence the policy agendas of the chief justices.

Chapter 5 completes this book's analysis, as we explore how chief justices navigate the state political environment to lead the state judiciary. Specifically, we examine the determinants of chief justices' successes or failures as advocates for their justice systems. Our results indicate that ideological proximity between a chief justice and state policymakers is significant for judicial advocacy efforts, as is the scope of the desired reform. Chapter 5 demonstrates that politics are never far removed from a chief justice's work.

Taken as a whole, this book informs readers about the characteristics and structures of state judicial leaders, analyzes the impact of those structures on chief justices, and examines the activities used by chiefs to improve state justice systems. We demonstrate that chief justices are often entangled with state politics, whether via judicial selection or through their dependence on a state's political leaders to enact reforms. We show that chief justices have grown accustomed to their administrative and political roles and frequently view them as their primary duties. Our goal for this research is to encourage a broader view of modern court leaders as vital players in state politics.

PART 1

CHAPTER 1

The Chief Justice as Institution

In February of 1993, Governor Mario M. Cuomo nominated Associate Judge Judith S. Kaye to be Chief Judge of the New York Court of Appeals.[1] Kaye had been the first woman to join that court when she was appointed (also by Cuomo) in 1983. Judge Kaye was 54 years old when she became chief judge, young enough to serve a full 14-year term (and then some) before reaching New York's mandatory judicial retirement age of 70. She assumed her leadership position eager to advance "positive social change" and "spearhead initiatives that would improve the efficacy of the state courts and the experience of New Yorkers." The new chief judge believed she could promote both goals because the position came with dual roles—the head of the New York Court of Appeals and leader of the state judiciary (Kaye 2019, 57). She ultimately became the longest serving chief judge in New York history and led the state's courts through meaningful reforms concerning access to justice, alternative dispute resolution, jury service, accountability courts, courthouse technology, and more. She also steered successful efforts to build new court facilities and improve the quality of existing judicial infrastructure (Kaye 2019; Lippman 2009).

Kaye's path to become New York's highest judicial officer was determined by a process outlined in Article VI of the state's constitution. In New York, governors select judicial nominees from a list of candidates assembled by the state's Commission on Judicial Nomination (Bliven 1993); these nominees must be confirmed by the state senate. While a handful of states besides New York use gubernatorial appointments to select court leaders, others use popular elections, peer vote, rotation, promotion of the most senior judge, or another selection mechanism. These institutional rules clearly influence who will get the job of court leader. For example, if New York's chief judge were chosen by seniority, Acting Chief Judge Richard D. Simons would have become chief instead of Judith Kaye. Simons was appointed eight months prior to Kaye in 1983. Her record-breaking tenure as the leader of New York's courts was facilitated by the state's 14-year terms for judges but constrained by its mandatory retirement age. Like selection methods, term length and tenure limits of chief justices and chief judges differ by state. How a state structures its tenure rules for chief justices can produce anything from short-term occupants of the position to entrenched incumbents.

This chapter explores the institutional design of chief justice selection and tenure. We provide summary information about the ways in which states select, keep, and replace their chief justices. Variation in the selection and tenure of state chief justices has a substantial impact on who occupies these positions and on their relationship to the state political environment. We also explore state-specific idiosyncrasies that are rarely acknowledged in studies of judicial selection. Our analysis reveals an important consideration. Specifically, we find that no matter what rules a state adopts for chief justice selection and tenure, politics are never removed from the activities of court leaders. In fact, how a state selects, replaces, and responds to its chief justice is often an overt reflection of the state political environment.

Chief Justice Selection

In the modern era, each state court of last resort is led by a "first among equals" tasked with court leadership and stewardship of the state justice system.[2] The leader of the court may be called "chief judge" (in Maryland and New York), "presiding judge" (in the Oklahoma Court of Criminal Appeals and Texas Court of Criminal Appeals), or "chief justice" (in all other states). Leadership responsibilities for the office vary but generally include judicial, managerial, and administrative functions not shared with other members of the state judiciary or colleagues on the state high court.[3] There is wide variation in how the individuals who serve in the role approach their duties. A key reason for this is the variety of ways lawyers, judges, associate justices, or politicians become chief justices. Some individuals seek the chief justiceship, often with particular goals in mind for court reform or legal outcomes. Some are chosen for the leadership role and agree to take the reins. Others may or may not have designs on the office and acquire the role via seniority or regular rotation among high court members.

The current methods used to select chief justices are summarized in table 1.1. Consistent with the notion that states serve as "laboratories of democracy," at least nine distinct methods are used to pick leaders of state high courts. At present, the most common way these courts choose their leaders is via the court itself. In 22 states, the members of the state high court vote among themselves to select a chief justice. In 13 states, governors are responsible for selecting the high court leader. The governor's choice may or may not be constrained by a judicial nomination commission that limits who the governor can choose or whether the governor's selection is approved. In 7 states, chief justices are chosen using either partisan or nonpartisan elections whereby citizens decide who will lead the state judiciary. In 4 states, the most senior member of the state's high court becomes chief justice and retains that seat while in active status.

The other four methods used to pick court leaders are more idiosyncratic, each utilized in only one state. In North Dakota, the chief is selected by a vote of the state high court and district court judges. In South Carolina, the chief is elected by the state legislature. In Indiana, the chief justice is selected by a judicial nominating commission (without the governor's formal involvement). In Nevada, the position is rotated by seniority.

Where chief justice selection is led by the judiciary, controversy is less common but is apparent from time to time. Chief justice selection that involves nonjudicial actors tends to spur more dissension and competition. Given the powers and prestige of court leaders, the means by which a state chooses its chief justice is occasionally subject to debate or revision. Related deliberations are often the result of strategic maneuvering by political leaders who want an ideological ally to lead the state's court system. Changes to the chief justice selection process can have meaningful consequences for judicial administration, as court leaders bring their own sets of goals and priorities to the position.

In the sections that follow, we provide information and illustrative examples for each method of selection. Most of the practices and individuals we discuss here are not well known but merit further examination, particularly as chief justices have become important administrative leaders and as states continue to (re)consider how they select chief jus-

Table 1.1. Selection Methods and Term Lengths of State Court Leaders, 2021

State	Selection method	Term (years)	State	Selection method	Term (years)
AL	PE	6	MT	NPE	8
AK	PV	3	NE	GOV[f]	Duration
AZ	PV	5	NV	ROT[g]	Rotation by seniority
AR	NPE	8	NH	GOV[e]	Until age 70
CA	GOV[a]	12	NJ	GOV[d]	7, then until age 70
CO	PV	10	NM	PV	2
CT	GOV[b]	8	NY	GOV[d]	14
DE	GOV[c]	12	NC	PE	8
FL	PV	2	ND	JUD	5
GA	PV	4	OH	NPE[h]	6
HI	GOV[d]	10	OK	PV[i]	2
ID	PV	4	OR	PV	6
IL	PV	3	PA	SEN	Duration
IN	JNC	5	RI	GOV[c]	During good behavior
IA	PV	8	SC	LEG	10
KS	SEN	Duration	SD	PV	4
KY	PV	4	TN	PV	4, then 2
LA	SEN	Duration	TX	PE[i]	6
ME	GOV[b]	7	UT	PV	4
MD	GOV	Until age 70	VT	GOV[c]	6
MA	GOV[e]	Until age 70	VA	PV	4
MI	PV	2	WA	PV	4
MN	NPE	6	WV	PV	1
MS	SEN	Duration	WI	PV	2
MO	PV	2	WY	PV	4

Source: Information from *The Book of the States*, 2021, published by The Council of State Governments (see 193–94). Although *The Book of the States* indicates that Georgia chief justices serve six-year terms, they actually serve four-year terms (Associated Press 2018, Tucker 2021).

Note: PV = peer vote, GOV = gubernatorial appointment, JNC = judicial nominating commission, JUD = election by supreme and district judges, LEG = legislative appointment, NPE = nonpartisan election, PE = partisan election, ROT = rotation by seniority, and SEN = seniority.

[a] With consent of the Commission on Judicial Appointments.
[b] With consent of the legislature.
[c] From JNC with consent of the legislature.
[d] From JNC with consent of the senate.
[e] With consent of the executive council.
[f] From JNC.
[g] Most senior justice by commission; lot in cases of tied seniority.
[h] Chosen in a partisan primary but a nonpartisan general election.
[i] Same method for both courts of last resort (state supreme court and court of criminal appeals).

tices and chief judges. Importantly, we find that no method used to select chief justices is altogether removed from state politics.

PEER VOTE

Members of the state high court elect a chief justice from the court's roster in a peer vote system. Most chief justices elected by their courts serve for a single term of predetermined length (a range of 2–10 years; mean = 3.96). In many states using the peer process, it is subject to long-standing norms that influence which justice is chosen. Still, there are occasions when justices make exceptions or break from precedent.

The Florida Supreme Court is an example of a high court that historically followed a regular practice in peer voting. A new chief justice was chosen by peer vote every two years, with a norm of choosing the next justice in order of seniority. The court strayed from this norm in 2016, when its members reelected Chief Justice Jorge Labarga to a second two-year term. Labarga was the first Florida chief justice to serve two consecutive terms since 1865. The stated explanation for his reelection was that his likely successor would reach mandatory retirement age within the next term, while all remaining justices had already served as chief (Kennedy 2016). More recently, the Florida Supreme Court elected Chief Justice Charles T. Canady for two consecutive terms ending in June 2022 (Florida Supreme Court 2019, 2022). While Florida had consistently rotated its peer-chosen chief justice for 150 years, the South Dakota Supreme Court reelected David E. Gilbertson as chief every four years from 2001 to 2017, with his tenure ending in January 2021. Gilbertson's five terms as chief justice are unprecedented in that state's history. Such prolonged tenure as chief is unusual but possible where justices control the process.

Illinois chief justices are elected by peer vote for three-year terms, with unwritten rules preferring the most senior justice who has not yet served as chief (Lupton 2022). Since the late 1960s, that system has elevated at least two chief justices who were quickly embroiled in controversy (Alfini, Gupta-Brietzke, and McMartin 2007). Chief Justice Roy J. Solfisburg Jr. resigned from the court in 1969 when he was accused of accepting stock from a corporation with litigation before the court. In 1997, Chief Justice James D. Heiple was censured by the Illinois Courts Commission for disobeying police and misusing his power to avoid traffic tickets, and he faced impeachment proceedings in the state legislature. Heiple's colleagues met to consider his removal but were one vote short of revoking his position (Armstrong and Pearson 1997). He resigned the chief justiceship soon afterward but remained an associate justice and served on the court until 2000.

On rare occasions, judicial control over chief justice selection leads to unusual outcomes or even necessary corrective action. West Virginia's Allen H. Loughry II was involved in both situations. Three months after Loughry began service as chief justice in January 2017, his colleagues changed court rules to extend his term to four years, deviating from a century of single-year tenures for West Virginia chief justices. Up to that point, no chief justice in West Virginia had served four consecutive years since 1888. The high court explained the rule change as recognizing the extensive duties of chief justices and serving a need for "efficient and competent administration of West Virginia's entire court system" through longer terms for judicial leaders (White 2017). Loughry's shot at a record-breaking tenure was short-lived, however. Less than a year later, his colleagues removed him from leadership while he was involved in a scandal involving fraud and misuse of state funds. Loughry, who rose to prominence as the author of a book about political corruption in West Virginia, was convicted of 11 federal crimes and sentenced to two years in prison in November 2018 (Kabler 2019; Pierson 2018).

GUBERNATORIAL APPOINTMENT

In states where governors appoint chief justices, most are constrained by the state legislature, executive council, or judicial nominating commission that participates in the process. Nonetheless, chief executives have a central role in these appointments and exercise meaningful influence on who will lead the state judiciary. Governors tend to select chief justices who share their ideological predispositions, just as American presidents do at the federal level. Chief justices appointed by governors tend to have relatively long terms (from 6 years to "life" tenure), including the entire remaining duration of the judge's service in Nebraska and Rhode Island. Of course, governors (like presidents) approach the task of appointment with different strategies and experience various levels of success.

The history of the California Supreme Court provides an illustrative example. Six governors of the Golden State appointed chief justices from the mid-1960s to the 2010s. Each picked a chief justice of shared political alignment. Democratic Governor Edmund G. "Pat" Brown elevated veteran justice Roger J. Traynor to the position in 1964. Traynor had been on the high court nearly a quarter century and was renowned for his bold "judicial creativity" and for common-law jurisprudence often resulting in liberal outcomes (Poulos 1995; Scheiber 2013, 2016). When then-governor Ronald Reagan had a chance to appoint a chief justice in 1970, he selected Republican appellate judge Donald R. Wright. Reagan's goal was to install a conservative leader to curb the liberal activism of the Traynor court. Wright's record as chief, particularly in criminal justice, disappointed Reagan, who called Wright his "biggest mistake" (Scheiber 2016). Democratic governor Jerry Brown selected Rose E. Bird as chief justice in 1977. Bird had served in Brown's cabinet and had no judicial experience. She was narrowly confirmed by a 2–1 vote (Scheiber 2016) and faced opposition from California conservatives throughout her tenure. When conservative governor George Deukmejian picked Bird's replacement in 1987, he elevated his former law partner and supreme court appointee Malcolm M. Lucas. Deukmejian was likely pleased with the result, as Lucas shifted the court toward the political right (Egelko 2016). Governor Pete B. Wilson also elevated one of his own supreme court appointees to the chief justiceship in 1996, when he chose Ronald M. George. The two had a long history of collaboration and shared political conservatism (Katches 1996). When George retired, then-governor Arnold Schwarzenegger selected Tani G. Cantil-Sakauye as George's successor in 2011. She was perceived as a fellow centrist Republican in line with the governor's own political leanings (Mintz 2010).

Each of these California governors chose a court leader with whom they were politically and personally compatible. All their chosen court leaders shared their ideological leanings, and several had close personal relationships with the relevant governor. Nonetheless, in at least one instance—Reagan's selection of Chief Justice Wright—a governor was later displeased by his appointment, a disappointment reminiscent of American presidents' occasional dissatisfaction with their own judicial appointments.[4]

Not obvious in the California example is that the constraints associated with consenting institutions are real. In states where governors cannot act unilaterally, they risk having their nominees for chief justice rejected. For example, New Hampshire governor Chris Sununu nominated Attorney General Gordon J. MacDonald to become chief justice in 2019. MacDonald had substantial experience as a litigator and government attorney but had never been a judge. He also had a long history of involvement in Republican politics (Rogers and Ganley 2021).[5] His nomination was rejected 3–2 by New Hampshire's elected Executive Council in 2019, when Democratic councilors held a slim majority. The council's majority expressed concern about MacDonald's lack of judicial experience and perceived conservatism. What followed can only be described as political brinksmanship. Governor Sununu criticized MacDonald's treatment as "hyperpartisan" and damaging to the state's process of judicial selection. He announced that he would pause all judicial nominations temporarily due to dissatisfaction with the Executive Council's judgments (Sununu 2019). Sununu left the chief justice position vacant until a new Executive Council was seated in 2021, with a 4–1 Republican majority. Once the new GOP majority was established in January 2021, MacDonald's nomination was confirmed, and he became chief justice (Wade 2021).

POPULAR ELECTIONS (PARTISAN OR NONPARTISAN)

Popular elections are the most visible selection mechanisms for chief justice seats. Where this form of selection is used, candidates for the position declare themselves and run in (potentially) competitive elections, with the voting public deciding the outcome. Winners in the elections remain or become chief justice regardless of their previous judicial experience or administrative acumen. For better or worse, voters pick the leader of the state court system using whatever criteria they see fit. This selection mechanism resulted in the nonconsecutive terms of Roy Moore as chief justice in Alabama despite his truncated first tenure. The term lengths for popularly elected chief justices range from 6 to 8 years (mean = 6.86). These court leaders can be reelected if they have not reached the state's mandatory retirement age.

Popular elections for chief justice seats are not common in the United States. In the 1950s, 12 of the 48 states used popular elections to pick chief justices. The number declined to 7 states by 1990. Nonpartisan elections for chief justice are used in Arkansas, Minnesota, and Montana, and partisan elections are used in Alabama, North Carolina, and Texas. Ohio used a hybrid system before 2022, with partisan primaries followed by a nonpartisan election. As of November 2022, both primary and general elections for Ohio appellate judges feature party labels (Borchardt 2021). Incumbent status is shown on the ballot of chief justice candidates in nonpartisan elections, but no cues related to party affiliation are provided to voters. In states with partisan elections for chief justices, candidates are clearly identified as affiliated with a specific political party.

In some states, popular elections for chief justices seldom lead to competitive elections. In Minnesota, for example, the more common series of events involves incumbent chief justices leaving office before their terms expire, allowing governors to appoint their replacements.[6] North Carolina maintained a similar norm for much of the 20th century, with Democratic governors routinely picking copartisan chief justices (Hayes 2008, 336). Chief justice elections in other states are sometimes less tranquil, with voters occasionally rejecting incumbents in favor of their challengers. When incumbents face challengers, their most common electoral foes are judges from lower courts. Sometimes, associate justices challenge their own incumbent chief justice (Vining, Wilhelm, and Wanless 2019). This phenomenon has occurred occasionally at least since Carl V. Weygandt, chief justice of the Ohio Supreme Court, was defeated by an associate justice, Kingsley A. Taft, in 1962.[7]

Several recent partisan elections for Alabama's chief justice generated controversy and concern among advocates for judicial selection reform. Much of that interest was related to the activities of Roy Moore (mentioned in the introduction) and Tom Parker, another conservative Republican judge. Moore's activism and rhetoric promoting religion in public life helped him defeat Harold F. See Jr., the Republican establishment's preferred candidate, in the 2000 primary. He then defeated Democratic appeals court judge Sharon G. Yates in the general election. After Moore became chief justice and then was removed from that position, voters elected him as chief justice again in 2012. During his second court run, he unseated incumbent chief justice Charles R. Malone in the primary before beating Circuit Judge Robert S. Vance Jr. in the general election.

In both 2006 and 2018, Justice Tom Parker entered the Republican primary attempting to unseat a chief justice from his own political party. Parker's effort to oust incumbent Chief Justice Drayton Nabers Jr. in 2006 was unsuccessful. He challenged Nabers with the intent of steering the Alabama courts toward defiance of federal court rulings that he viewed as objectionable. Parker later defeated incumbent Chief Justice Lyn Stuart in the June 2018 Republican primary despite the opposition of several current and former Alabama Supreme Court justices who endorsed Stuart's retention. Stuart emphasized her focus on judicial administration, explaining that "the role of chief justice" is "doing what's best for the entire court system, rather than having a personal agenda." Parker contended that his leadership would be better than hers at a "pivotal point" when the U.S. Supreme Court's conservative wing needed "cases that they can use to reverse what the liberal majorities have done in the past" (Brown 2018). Parker also argued that his experience lobbying Alabama legislators for conservative policies would aid his efforts to achieve administrative goals of the state courts, including greater funding (Brown 2018). After winning the GOP primary, Parker defeated Robert S. Vance Jr. in the partisan general election.

Three of the seven states that hold elections for their chief justices, Arkansas, North Carolina, and Ohio, switched between partisan and nonpartisan elections since 2000. Arkansas began using nonpartisan judicial elections in 2002 after the adoption of Amendment 80, a constitutional revision approved by voters (Kritzer 2020, 69–74). North Carolina shifted from nonpartisan to partisan supreme court elections in 2018.[8] As mentioned above, Ohio moved from nonpartisan to partisan Supreme Court elections in 2022.

SENIORITY

In Kansas, Louisiana, Mississippi, and Pennsylvania, the chief justice is determined as a result of seniority. A fifth state, Wisconsin, chose its chief justice by seniority until 2015. In these states, the judge with the longest tenure on the high court serves as chief justice for that judge's entire remaining period of service. Notably, this method of selection facilitated the elevation of both the longest-serving chief justice in American history (Sydney M. Smith of Mississippi) and the first Black chief justice (Robert N. C. Nix Jr. of Pennsylvania). Both justices likely benefited from the determinative nature of elevation by seniority, with no opportunity for peers or politicians to influence who is promoted to the leadership post.

Lawmakers are presumably aware of the benefits and consequences associated with choosing chief justices by seniority. History demonstrates that state legislators wishing to unseat a disfavored chief judge and facilitate the ascension of a perceived ally will occasionally adopt or eliminate the selection of chief justices by seniority. Such an event occurred in Kansas more than a century ago. During the 1898 election, Kansas voters handed control of the legislature to Republicans and approved a constitutional amendment to expand the state high court from three to seven members. Within the amendment was a provision inserted by Republicans weary of the current chief justice's leadership. The provision shifted the selection of chief justices from a popular vote to seniority of continued service, a change that meant Republican justice William A. Johnston would become chief justice once the amendment was effective (Moline 1987). The intention of the provision was clear at the time, as there "was never much doubt that the amendment had been carefully crafted for Johnston's benefit" (Moline 1987, 23). Johnston became chief justice in 1903 and held the seat until 1935, serving over 50 years on the Kansas Supreme Court. The reform initiated to benefit Johnston has persisted, and the Kansas high court still designates chief justices based on seniority.

While Kansas Republicans established selection by seniority to facilitate the promotion of an ally, Wisconsin Republicans abolished a seniority system in 2015 so they could unseat a perceived foe. Shirley S. Abrahamson, a left-leaning Democratic appointee, had served as a justice of the Wisconsin high court since 1976 and became its chief justice in 1996 as a result of her seniority (Marley 2015).[9] By 2011, Republicans had won control of the state legislature and the governor's office and had a 4–3 majority on the state's high court. While Abrahamson remained in office, they were unable to secure the chief justice position. Tensions between Abrahamson and her Republican colleagues on the Wisconsin Supreme Court were widely publicized. For instance, it was broadly reported that Justice David T. Prosser Jr. had called Abrahamson a "total bitch" during an argument in 2010 (Elbow 2011).

Whether in response to partisan impulses, genuine concern about Abrahamson's leadership, or some combination of the two, Wisconsin Republicans introduced a constitutional amendment in 2011 to change the selection method of the chief justice from seniority to peer vote (Elbow 2011). Republicans framed the seniority system as out of date and detrimental to collegiality, while Democrats argued that the bill was "a purely political attack on Chief Justice Shirley Abrahamson" (D. Hall 2013). After the amendment was passed twice by the legislature on party-line votes, voters approved it in April 2015 by a margin of 53 to 47 percent (Marley 2015). Within hours after the election returns were certified, the court's four conservatives elected Patience D. Roggensack as chief justice over the objections of their left-leaning colleagues (Bauer 2015). Abrahamson challenged her deposal in federal court, arguing that she should be able to serve as chief justice until the end of her term, in 2019. Her challenge was unsuccessful (Beck 2015; Strebel 2015), and she served her remaining years on the court as an associate justice.

JUDICIAL NOMINATING COMMISSION

While several states use a judicial nominating commission to assist governors with the selection of chief justices, Indiana is the lone state that delegates the responsibility for picking the supreme court's leader to a commission. The Hoosier State's judicial nominating commission was established in the early 1970s and consists of three attorneys, three non-lawyers, and the state's chief justice or a justice designated by the chief justice to serve. The members other than the chief justice (or the chief justice's designee) are appointed by the governor. The Indiana Constitution requires that the commission pick chief justices to serve for five-year terms. That system is usually congenial and relatively private. However, at least one notable exception reveals the potential for discontent when an outside body is tasked with picking the chief justice.

In 1987, Richard M. Givan resigned as chief justice to return to service as an associate justice. Givan announced his support for Alfred J. Pivarnik to be chief justice. Pivarnik was a fellow Republican with 10 years of service on the high court. After completing deliberations, the commission selected Randall T. Shepard for the chief justiceship. Shepard was 40 years old at the time, with less than 18 months of service on the court. Givan reiterated that he "would have liked them to have chosen Al," and Pivarnik told journalists that he was "shocked" by the outcome (Ashley 1987).

The following year, Pivarnik accused Shepard of engaging in alcohol abuse, drug use, and possible homosexual activity prior to becoming chief justice. Pivarnik alleged that the judicial nominating commission and the governor, Robert D. Orr, had conspired to conceal incriminating information about Shepard (Grass 1988). The allegations led to substantial media coverage, intracourt strife, and exasperated responses from Governor Orr (Grass 1988; Associated Press 1988). While a police investigation concluded that the salacious claims were "rumors and innuendos that cannot be substantiated" (Associated Press 1988), Givan and Pivarnik continued to make accusatory statements to journalists. Nonetheless, the Indiana Supreme Court was reported to be functional and relatively collegial while Shepard led a court including his accusers (Associated Press 1989). Shepard went on to serve five terms as chief justice.

ROTATION

Nevada is the only state that formally uses regular rotation in the chief justice position. The Nevada Supreme Court's rules dictate that the chief justice is "the Justice whose current commission is senior in the date of its issuance," with the chief justice determined "by lot" in the event of a tie.[10] As a result, the chief is typically the justice with the least time remaining in a six-year term on the bench. When an incumbent justice is reelected, that justice reverts to being the least-senior justice for the purposes of choosing the court's leader. There is a regular reshuffling of seniority as justices are elected and reelected to the court. Justices who serve prolonged tenures tend to become chief justice multiple times, moving in and out of the leadership role with the passage of election cycles.[11]

LEGISLATIVE SELECTION

A single state, South Carolina, requires that the chief justice be selected by a joint assembly of the state legislature. Once selected, chief justices serve 10-year terms. By tradition, the legislature elevates the longest-serving member of the court to lead the judiciary (Bryant 1988). The state legislature even respected that tradition in 1994, when the state's judicial retirement age meant that Chief Justice Archie Lee Chandler would only serve five months in the position (Greene 1994). Interestingly, the tradition facilitated the elevation of South Carolina's first Black and female chief justices, in 1994 and 2000, when Ernest A. Finney Jr. and Jean Hoefer Toal were the court's longest-serving associate justices. There have been multiple efforts by Republican state legislators to challenge this norm since 2014, but they have failed to buck tradition as of 2022.[12]

ELECTION BY THE SUPREME COURT AND DISTRICT JUDGES

North Dakota has used a unique method to select a chief justice since 1967 (Holewa 2009), with members of the state supreme court and of the state's district courts voting for the position. Members of the state supreme court announce themselves as candidates, and ballots are distributed to the judges eligible to vote. The judges return the ballots, which are then tallied by the state court administrator. If no justice receives a majority vote in the initial balloting, the top two candidates proceed to a runoff election (Dura 2019). The elected chief justice serves a five-year term and is then eligible for reelection, which frequently occurs. Just two men were chief justice of North Dakota from 1973 to 2019, Ralph J. Erickstad (1973–92) and Gerald W. VandeWalle (1993–2019). The state legislature adopted the current system of chief justice selection to facilitate skilled, stable judicial leadership (Meschke and Smith 2000), a goal largely achieved.

Chief Justice Tenure

Once individuals become chief justices, there is substantial variation in the durations of their stays in the office. Some of the differences are explained by the various tenure rules and term lengths employed by the states. The practical impact of variation in these rules is that some chief justices have opportunities to serve long tenures while others do not. Where short-term chief justices are the norm, leaders are unlikely to have the long-range plans or deep impact of chief justices who are more entrenched.

Randall T. Shepard, chief justice in Indiana from 1987 to 2012, noted that how long chiefs serve has important implications for the style and impact of their leadership:

> When I first began attending . . . meetings of chief justices, I was struck by how often the members asked each other the method by which they had been chosen as chief. The long list of variations made for an interesting wrinkle on the idea of the states as laboratories of democracy. After a few dozen such conversations, I began to notice that the crowd also broke down along a different line. Because some states change their chief justice every year or every other year, new arrivals to the crowd rise up to middle seniority in short order. There were short-timers and long-timers. Later yet, I came to the realization that there were certain members who were just passing through, capping off their legal careers by sitting center chair in their home state, and others of obvious gravitas who approached their task purposefully on both the state and national scene. Put another way, there were some who just wanted to be the leader and others who wanted to lead somewhere. (Shepard 2009b, 671)

Shepard's observations have substantial merit. Extended tenure gives a chief justice an enhanced opportunity to leave a mark on the state judiciary.

As of 2021, 42 chief justices, listed in table 1.2, have served for at least 20 years. Two Delaware chief justices with long tenures, Kensey Johns Sr. and James Booth Sr., served concurrently. Under the state's 1792 constitution, both held the title of chief justice, and their separate state courts were of relatively equal standing (Grubb 1894, 356–57). Charles N. Potter accumulated nearly 21 years of service as Wyoming chief justice across four stints over a 29-year period (1897–1927). His unusual tenure was possible because Wyoming then rotated the leadership position among its three justices, designating the "justice having the shortest term to serve and not holding his office by appointment or election to fill a vacancy" as chief justice (Bell 1908–9, 178). One of the long-tenured chief justices, William Beatty, led the high courts of two states.[13] Beatty served as chief justice of the Nevada Supreme Court from 1879 until his term expired in January 1881. He then returned to private practice in Sacramento, California, and was elected to the California Supreme Court in 1889.[14] Beatty was reelected repeatedly and served as chief justice of California until 1914.

Many long-serving chief justices are among the best-known or most influential jurists from their respective states. Several chief judges with extended tenures were leaders in judicial administration or judicial reform. For example, John Appleton of Maine worked to reform the law of evidence (Gold 1990) and John B. Fournet of Louisiana oversaw the midcentury reorganization of his state's appellate courts and established its modern system of court administration (Billings 1997, 460).

The longest tenure among states' chief justices was served by Sydney M. Smith on the Mississippi Supreme Court from 1912 to 1948. Smith's nearly 36 years as his court's leader surpassed the 34 years served as chief justice by John Marshall of the U.S. Supreme Court from 1801 to 1835. When Robert B. Mayes resigned the chief post, Smith became chief justice due to seniority despite having served only three years. Smith was 43 years old at the time. Beginning in 1916, he retained the seat via popular elections every eight years, with the Democratic primary being the sole meaningful contest in the one-party Mississippi of that era (Southwick 1997). Smith's challengers included a former Mississippi governor in 1916 and chancery court judges in 1932 and 1940. He declined to run in 1948 due to poor health following a heart attack (Southwick 1997, 152).[15]

Five other state chief justices served at least 30 years in the position, and 10 more were chief justices for at least 25 years. Very few modern chief justices have such longevity, whether due to institutional rules, mandatory retirement, elevation to another office, or electoral defeat.

Table 1.2. Individuals Serving 20 Years or More as State Court Leaders, 1776–2021

Time as Chief	State	Chief Justice	Period	Commission method
35 years, 11 mos.	MS	Sydney M. Smith	1912–48	Seniority
32 years, 11 mos.	NJ	Mercer Beasley	1864–97	Appointed by governor
32 years, 5 mos.	KS	William A. Johnston	1903–35	Seniority
31 years, 5 mos.	DE	Kensey Johns Sr.	1799–1830	Appointed by governor
31 years, 2 mos.	NJ	William S. Gummere	1901–33	Appointed by governor
30 years	OH	Carl V. Weygandt	1933–62	Elected
29 years, 11 mos.	MA	Lemuel Shaw	1830–60	Appointed by governor
29 years	DE	James Booth Sr.	1799–1828	Appointed by governor
27 years, 7 mos.	NE, CA	William Beatty[a]	1879–80, 1889–1914	Rotation NV, elected CA
27 years	MD	Benjamin Rumsey	1778–1806	Appointed by general assembly
27 years	ND	Gerald W. VandeWalle	1993–2019	Peer vote
26 years, 9 mos.	MA	Arthur P. Rugg	1911–1938	Appointed by governor
26 years, 8 mos.	LA	Charles A. O'Niell	1922–49	Seniority
26 years, 3 mos.	AL	John C. Anderson	1914–40	Appointed by governor
25 years, 6 mos.	NH	Frank R. Kenison	1952–77	Appointed by governor
25 years, 1 mo.	IN	Randall T. Shepard	1987–2012	Appointed by judicial nominating commission
24 years, 7 mos.	PA	John B. Gibson	1827–51	Appointed by governor
24 years, 2 mos.	CA	Phil S. Gibson	1940–64	Appointed by governor
24 years, 2 mos.	MD	Robert C. Murphy	1972–96	Appointed by governor
24 years	NE	Robert G. Simmons	1939–63	Appointed by governor
23 years, 11 mos.	DE	James Pennewell	1909–33	Appointed by governor
23 years, 9 mos.	TN	Grafton Green	1923–47	Peer vote
23 years, 8 mos.	MT	Theodore Brantly	1899–1922	Elected

Table 1.2—*Continued*

Time as Chief	State	Chief Justice	Period	Commission method
23 years, 8 mos.	AR	Carleton Harris	1957–80	Elected
23 years, 4 mos.	LA	George Mathews Jr.	1813–36	Seniority
23 years, 3 mos.	OH	Thomas J. Moyer	1987–2010	Elected
22 years, 8 mos.	ID	Joseph J. McFadden	1959–82	Appointed by governor
22 years, 4 mos.	PA	Thomas McKean	1777–99	Appointed by state president (governor)
22 years, 3 mos.	RI	Edmund W. Flynn	1935–57	Elected by grand committee of the House and Senate
22 years, 2 mos.	NH	Frank N. Parsons	1902–24	Appointed by governor
21 years, 8 mos.	NH	William M. Richardson	1816-38	Appointed by governor
21 years, 5 mos.	VA	James Keith	1895–1916	Peer vote
21 years, 4 mos.	NC	Walter M. Clark	1903–24	Elected
21 years, 2 mos.	PA	William Tilghman	1806–27	Appointed by governor
21+	TX	Sharon Keller	2001–present	Elected
20 years, 11 mos.	ME	John Appleton	1862–83	Appointed by governor
20 years, 11 mos.	GA	William H. Duckworth	1948–69	Peer vote
20 years, 10 mos.	LA	John B. Fournet	1949–70	Seniority
20 years, 10 mos.	WY	Charles N. Potter[b]	1897–1903, 1905–11, 1915–19, 1920–27	Rotation by seniority
20 years, 10 mos.	WI	Marvin B. Rosenberry	1929–50	Seniority
20 years, 1 mo.	MN	James Gilfillan	1869–70, 1875–94	Appointed by governor (both terms)
20 years	SD	David E. Gilbertson	2001-21	Peer vote

[a] William Beatty served as chief justice for 2 years in Nevada and for 25 years and 7 months in California.

[b] Charles N. Potter served four stints as chief justice, by rotation via seniority on the three-member Wyoming Supreme Court.

Only six state court leaders who began their tenures after 1970 served for 20 years or longer.[16]

Research on the Impact of Institutional Rules

Chief justice selection and tenure are inherently influenced by the politics of a particular place. Political elites establish the rules used to pick court leaders. Those rules provide a structure that influences which individuals become judicial leaders as well as their likely impacts on the courts. While the historical evidence presented above suggests that chief justice selection is often intertwined with state politics, empirical analyses allow us to identify broader trends regarding the implications of chief justice selection and tenure rules.

PREVIOUS RESEARCH

When scholars have examined the role of politics in the selection of chief justices, they have most often focused on peer voting. Election by the court allows intracourt politics to influence who becomes chief justice when multiple candidates vie for the position. The results from studies of election within the court are mixed. Langer et al. (2003) found that ideologically extreme judges are less likely to be elected as chief justice by their peers. More recently, Fife, Goelzhauser, and Loertscher (2021) concluded that ideological tendencies are less influential than the rate at which a justice dissents from the court's decisions.

Researchers have also examined the dynamics of popular elections for chief justices. Vining, Wilhelm, and Wanless (2019) discovered that associate justices who challenge chief justices in elections tend to be distant ideologically from the chief and become candidates because they want to flip control of the court's leadership from one political faction to another. Building on that research, we provide a list of associate justice challengers from 1990 to 2020 in table 1.3. Of the seven associate justices who attempted to unseat a chief justice during that period, five were from the opposite party. An associate justice challenging the chief justice risks instigating intracourt conflict, and in many instances, this is exactly what happened. Still, the potential benefits are clear for an ambitious judge eager to steer the court in another direction. Four of the seven challengers were successful, most since 2000.

Table 1.3. Chief Justices Challenged by Associate Justices, 1990–2020

Year	State	Chief Justice (party)	Associate Justice (party)	Successful challenge
1990	TX	Thomas R. Phillips (R)	Oscar H. Mauzy (D)	No
1992	MT	Jean A. Turnage (R)	Terry N. Trieweiler (D)	No
2000	NC	Henry E. Frye (D)	I. Beverly Lake (R)	Yes
2006	AL	Drayton Nabers Jr. (R)	Tom Parker (R)	No
2010	OH	Eric S. Brown (D)	Maureen O'Connor (R)	Yes
2018	AL	Lyn Stuart (R)	Tom Parker (R)	Yes
2020	NC	Cheri L. Beasley (D)	Paul M. Newby (R)	Yes

Note: Adapted from Vining, Wilhelm, and Wanless 2019. Where judicial elections were formally nonpartisan, party affiliation determined by source of campaign donations.

A commonality in research on chief justice selection is each article's focus on a singular selection method. Langer et al. (2003) and Fife, Goelzhauser, and Loertscher (2021) help us understand the impact of ideology when the court chooses its leader. Vining, Wilhelm, and Wanless (2019) demonstrate the impact of ideology on chief justice selection when the public controls the outcome. But what about leaders chosen via other methods of selection? Are certain systems of chief justice selection more likely to result in certain kinds of leaders?

Langer and Wilhelm (2005) provide preliminary answers. In an analysis of state chief justices between 1970 and 2004, they found that those selected by the government or by the court itself were more liberal than chief justices chosen by other means. Perhaps surprisingly, they also found that the ideology of elected chief justices was not statistically different than those chosen by rotation or judicial commission. The analysis by Langer and Wilhelm helped provide a generalizable answer to the question of whether rules of chief justice selection influence the kind of individual who will become chief justice.

RESEARCH UPDATE

Given the time elapsed since the 2005 analysis by Langer and Wilhelm, we reexamined the relationship between selection systems and chief justice ideology. To do so, we compiled a complete list of chief justice selections that occurred in the states between 1970 and 2020. Because a chief justice could serve multiple terms in this model (i.e., could win another chief justice election, be reelected by peers, etc.), a chief justice may appear in the data multiple times. Our analysis includes 587 chief justice selections (with 541 unique chief justices). Our dependent variable is each chief justice's political ideology at the time of selection, as measured by scores of party-adjusted judge ideology (PAJID) that Brace, Langer, and Hall (2000) used to represent judicial ideology.[17]

Our independent variables include the median ideology of the state supreme court (also PAJID data), the political ideology of the state political elite, and the average political ideology of the state citizenry, all at the time of selection. We used data from Berry et al. (1998, 2013) to represent elite and citizen ideology. These measures are scaled on a common dimension with PAJID (0 is most conservative and 100 is most liberal). We also include systems of chief justice selection, categorized as peer vote (23 states), election (7 states), government appointment without commission (4 states), commission-assisted appointment (11 states), and rotation/seniority (5 states).[18] Given the censored nature of the dependent variable, our model is fit with tobit regression and includes fixed effects for state-level idiosyncrasies. Our results are shown in table 1.4. Positive coefficients indicate that chief justices are more liberal where a selection system is used, and negative coefficients are associated with court leaders who are more conservative.

While the results comport with earlier findings that selection methods are associated with certain chief justice ideologies, our substantive findings are quite different from prior research. Specifically, we find that chief justice elections produce chief justices that are significantly more conservative than their counterparts, as do systems of government appointment. We also find that chief justices chosen by peer vote or selection that incorporates judicial commissions are not ideologically different from chief justices chosen by other means. The differences in our findings may be explained by broader political trends and increased politicization of judicial elections in recent decades. For example, the states where chief justices are elected (Alabama, Arkansas, Minnesota, Montana, North Carolina, Ohio, and Texas) have generally become more supportive of Republican politicians since the 1990s. Meanwhile, several chief justices elected from those states were staunch conservatives (e.g., Nathan L. Hecht, Roy S. Moore, Paul M. Newby, and Tom Parker). The results for government-appointed chief justices (grouped for Connecticut, Maine, Maryland, and South Carolina) are not as transparent.

Like findings reported by Langer and Wilhelm, our results identify a significant and positive relationship between the ideology of the state's

Table 1.4. Selection Methods and Chief Justice Ideology, 1970–2020

	Coefficient	Standard error	Significance
Peer vote	3.43	7.24	
Election	−24.53	10.16	**
Government appointment (without commission)	−20.71	11.93	**
Commission/council	−1.62	25.16	
Rotation/seniority	*omitted*		
State citizen ideology	0.40	0.12	**
State elite ideology	1.43	0.10	**
Constant	−27.93	10.04	**

Note: $N = 515$; results calculated with tobit regression and fixed effects for each state.

chief justice and the ideology of the state citizenry and governmental elites. These results suggest that chief justices tend to be in step ideologically with their states, all else being equal, whether viewed through the lens of citizens or government officials. This relationship brings up an additional point of inquiry. Specifically, what might influence the ideological concordance between a chief justice and state citizens or government elites? More important, can a state's method of selecting a chief justice structure ideological proximity with the chief justice?

While not all procedures for chief justice selection empower one political actor or force over another, most clearly do. Peer vote systems give authority to the state supreme court to determine the next chief justice. Popular elections give voters the ability to pick the state's chief justice. Government-appointed systems delegate authority over selection to the governor or state legislature. We have already shown that some of those selection systems are associated with more liberal or conservative chief justices since the 1970s. Does the selection authority in those situations tend to select chief justices with whom it aligns ideologically? That is, do judges, voters, or other elites tend to select chief justices from their own political camps? The rationale behind an examination of that question is intuitive: if each empowered actor prefers a chief justice that is ideologically congruent, the individual selected as chief justice should reflect that preference. If specific systems of chief justice selection can engender greater ideological congruency, states with specific institutional goals in mind for their high court may want to take notice.

To determine whether systems of chief justice selection result in a closer ideological "match" between the chief justice and the empowered

Table 1.5. Selection Methods and Ideological Proximity with the Chief Justice, 1970–2020

	CJ–Court Distance	CJ–Citizen Distance	CJ–Gov Elite Distance
Peer vote	3.35	–1.5	–.42
	(7.98)	(3.48)	(3.02)
Election	–1.61	–7.41	7.41*
	(11.29)	(4.92)	(4.27)
Government appoint-	–11.27	–5.17	4.35
ment (without	(14.36)	(5.75)	(5.0)
commission)			
Commission	143.67	–23.04*	4.48
	(3,144.67)	(12.20)	(10.6)
Rotation/seniority	*omitted*	*omitted*	*omitted*
Constant	8.78	25.34*	16.13*
	(9.05)	(3.91)	(3.4)

Note: $*p < 0.05$; $N = 515$; results calculated with tobit regression and fixed effects for each state.

actor in the selection process, we again analyzed chief justices from 1970 to 2020. We investigated the impact of selection method on a chief justice's ideological proximity to other state political actors. The dependent variable in our analysis is the ideological distance between the chief justice and (separately) state citizenry, state governmental elites, and the state high court. We again used tobit regression models with state-level fixed effects. The results are presented in table 1.5.

We find no evidence that any selection system is particularly associated with congruence between the chief justice and the political actor(s) responsible for selection. None of our model estimates identify a significant link between a selection method and ideological proximity between chiefs and those who choose them. In fact, the only selection system associated with ideological congruence, operationalized here as lesser ideological distance and denoted by a significant negative coefficient, is the selection mechanism that incorporates a judicial nominating commission. That method of selecting the chief justice is associated with greater political congruence between the chief justice and state citizenry. However, the theoretical linkage in that situation is not as clear as it would be if voters tethered chief justices to public opinion. It is feasible that commissions perceive themselves as agents that choose judicial nominees in line with the public mood, but no such relationship is established in previous literature.

Conclusion

Our research into chief justice selection and tenure reveals that the methods used to pick court leaders are diverse, fluid, and consequential. In addition, we find that the selection of court leaders is often part of broader trends or conflicts in state politics. Political elites understand the importance of the chief justice position and its functions, and this understanding is often reflected in who is chosen to serve in the position.

That several methods are used to pick chief justices is unsurprising. After all, states use multiple selection processes to choose judges for their high courts. Chief justices may come from within the court or from outside its roster, depending on a state's legal guidelines. Methods of selection associated with random or short-term chief justices have fallen out of favor in many states, though some states still rely on seniority or rotation to designate chief justices. Elections for chief justice are now restricted to a handful of states and are sometimes the venue for quarrelsome contests for the job. Occasionally, elections even feature associate justices attempting to unseat a colleague (Vining, Wilhelm, and Wanless 2019). Most typical, however, are chief justices chosen by their colleagues or appointed by a governor and/or commission. Those court leaders are presumably vetted by their fellow judges or the appointing authority, though the potential for political influence exists (Langer et al. 2003) and is sometimes obvious.

Our statistical analyses in this chapter provide interesting insights regarding the impact of selection systems. Court leaders who are elected by citizens or chosen directly by government officials have been more conservative, on average, than those picked through other means. Interestingly, though, the general trend is for chief justices to have ideological tendencies like the states' political environment and leaders. This trend is consistent with our general thesis that chief justices are chosen and operate within a set of state-specific conditions. It is not surprising that the men and women who reach these leadership positions are politically in step with local voters and elites. Notably, our final analysis shows that the various selection systems do not differ much in their ability to limit the ideological distance between court leaders and the appointing authority. All of them do so at similar rates, though clearly via different pathways.

In this chapter, we have examined the different ways that chief justices are chosen and retained, as well as the impact of those institutional mechanisms on ideological tendencies. Of course, political ideology is just one characteristic of a chief justice's profile. The range of individuals who serve or have served as state court leaders is meaningful and varied. Like ideology, personal characteristics of a state's chief justice may say something about the state political environment itself. In chapter 2, we turn our attention to the kinds of individuals who serve in the chief justice position.

CHAPTER 2

The Chief Justice as Individual

Ernest A. Finney Jr. of South Carolina became chief justice of the Palmetto State's highest court in 1994 (Roberts 2017). He was the state's first African American supreme court justice since Jonathan Jasper Wright's tenure in the Reconstruction era. Finney's interesting path to court leadership included legal education at a segregated law school, experience as a teacher and civil rights attorney in the Jim Crow South, and service in the state House of Representatives. Finney also spent nine years as the state's first Black circuit judge and nine years as an associate justice on the state's highest court. He was elected to lead the high court by the state legislature, a selection method now unique to South Carolina. Finney's career path speaks to several aspects of modern chief justices and their backgrounds. His professional work gave him both legal and political experience, as well as prior opportunities for leadership roles. Additionally, his personal characteristics provided descriptive and symbolic representation (Pitkin 1967) for a group of South Carolina citizens historically marginalized.

How common or unique are the aspects of Finney's background in comparison to others who become chief justice? As explored in chapter 1, a state's institutional design for chief justice selection and tenure affects who gets chosen to lead state judiciaries and how long they do so. In addition, individuals who serve as chief justices are intrinsically linked to their state political environments. The institutional rules that prompt turnover and connect court leaders to statewide trends also influence the professional and personal backgrounds of court leaders.

It is likely that the different professional backgrounds of the chief justices factor into variations in their leadership abilities. For example, modern chief justices uniformly have training as attorneys and possess skills related to the legal profession. Most also served as judges before becoming chief justices. However, they tend to have less preparation related to extrajudicial responsibilities and vary in their abilities to navigate them, as well as their interest in doing so. Some professional backgrounds prepare chief justices for leadership, whether within the court or as liaison to the public and political elites. Individuals trained or socialized primarily in a judicial capacity may be less eager or prepared for the overtly political aspects of the job. Meanwhile, chief justices with political experience may be more enthusiastic about navigating interbranch relations or engaging in public discourse.

Variations in the personal characteristics of chief justices are similarly significant, given that they contribute to the diversity of judges and public perception of courts. Court leaders currently represent assorted groups in American society. However, diversity among chief justices is a relatively recent phenomenon. The judges of state high courts were almost all white men for the first two centuries of U.S. history. Women and members of minority racial and ethnic groups now occupy a substantial proportion of judgeships on state high courts. As that proportion grew, so did the number of diverse court leaders.

In this chapter, we provide a collective profile of the individuals who serve as state chief justices. We examine the backgrounds and experiences that may have consequences for a chief justice's job performance, professional ability, and perceptions of institutional legitimacy. We posit that success in the dual roles of the chief justice is influenced by the skill set and priorities individuals bring with them to the center seat, given that each court leader must manage the high court and the state judicial system. Sue Bell Cobb, chief justice of Alabama, remarked that being chief justice is "two full time jobs if you do it right" (Peck 2011).

We also focus this chapter's analysis on the diversity among state chief justices across the states. We examine whether particular selection mechanisms or state characteristics are associated with the ascension of diverse chief justices since the 1970s. Our findings indicate that diversification of the chief seat is associated more with statewide ideological conditions than with institutional rules.

Professional Experiences of Chief Justices

The career paths that individuals follow to become chief justices vary considerably. Many spend decades as judges before reaching the pinnacle of the state court system, while others reach the role of chief justice early in their judicial careers. For some, the chief position is their first judgeship. As a result, some new chief justices are well acquainted with their colleagues and the state's court system, while others have a steeper learning curve. Chief justices accustomed to coalition building, public advocacy, or administrative leadership may fare better in the role than those with less-developed skills in these areas.

JUDICIAL AND LEGAL EXPERIENCE

To understand the professional experience of state court leaders, we examined the backgrounds of chief justices who served from 1970 to 2021. We began our analysis using data from Goelzhauser (2016), which we updated through mid-2021.[1] In figure 1, we provide a summary of the prior professional positions held by the 541 court leaders we examined. Many individuals held more than one of these jobs during their professional careers.

The most common path to court leadership is, not surprisingly, a career in the judiciary. The vast majority (95.4 percent) of chief justices previously served as judges. This service is a given for chief justices who are elevated via seniority or election by the court. All 25 chief justices without previous judicial experience were either elected to the bench by the public or appointed by a governor or state legislature.

A nontrivial subset of chief justices served as prosecutors or attorneys general. This service is unsurprising given the close historical relationship between states' attorneys and the judiciary, with the prosecutor's office often perceived as a stepping stone to the courts. Attorneys general are also well situated to claim expertise regarding the court system. They are the top legal officers in state government, representing the interests of the citizenry and state. In our data, 7.8 percent of chief justices previously served as prosecutors at the local, state, or federal level, while 4.4 percent of chief justices previously served as attorneys general.

If the overwhelming tendency is for chief justices to have prior judicial experience, why are some individuals chosen as court leaders if they were

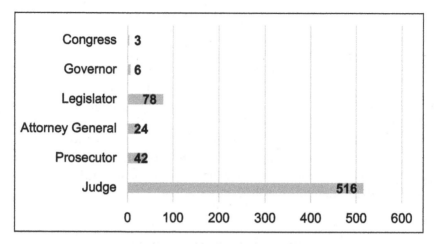

Fig. 1. Prior professional experiences of chief justices, 1970–2021. (*Note: N* = 541 chief justices; chiefs may appear in multiple categories.)

never judges? Table 2.1 lists individuals who became chief justice without prior judicial experience. The 25 chief justices who never previously served as judges are split between those appointed by a governor (*N* = 18), elected by the public (*N* = 6), or chosen via legislative election (*N* = 1).[2] The conditions associated with the selection of these chief justices underscore the impact that state politics can have on the judicial selection process.

Governors selected chief justices without judicial experience from a variety of backgrounds, but many of them had strong links to the state's political leadership. State chief executives picked four chief justices who had no judicial experience but who were the incumbent attorneys general from their respective states. Of those four individuals, three (Deborah T. Portitz, Stuart J. Rabner, and Gordon J. MacDonald) were appointed as attorneys general by the governor who picked them as chief justices. Other governors picked chief justices from individuals serving their administrations as lieutenant governor, legal counsel, cabinet member, state finance director, or chair of a judicial selection commission. Bradley D. Jesson of Arkansas and then-lieutenant governor William S. Richardson of Hawaii were appointed chief justices after earlier stints as Democratic Party chairs in their states. Robert N. Wilentz of New Jersey, who was appointed by Governor Brendan T. Byrne in 1979, served two terms in the state legislature and regularly participated in committees assembled by the state's governors (Stout 1996).

The remaining appointed chief justices without prior judicial experience have fewer obvious ties to governors, but all had distinguished legal careers. James T. Harrison and Michael G. Heavican were career prosecutors. Vincent L. McKusick and Frederic W. Allen were prestigious attorneys in their home states. Prior to selection as chief justice, Delaware's E. Norman Veasey, a onetime president of the state bar, was also a regular participant in committees assembled by the state's governors and supreme court (Horsey and Duffy 1993).

Two men appointed as chief justices who served as close informal advisors to governors were Webster L. Hubbell of Arkansas and Norman M. Krivosha of Nebraska. Hubbell was active in Little Rock politics, including a stint as mayor. As a close associate of then-governor Bill Clinton and his wife, Hillary Rodham Clinton, he provided them ample support in the drafting and passage of legislation. His appointment as chief justice in 1984 was temporary, and he vacated the position months later. Krivosha was unpaid counsel and advisor to Nebraska governor J. James Exon, who appointed him in December 1978. The two men were extremely tight (Hewitt 2007, 67). Krivosha served almost a decade in the chief justice position and had substantial administrative impact during his tenure.[3]

Many of the individuals without judicial experience who voters elected as chief justices were well-known figures in their respective states. Howell T. Heflin was the nephew of a former U.S. senator and was active in Alabama politics. Clement C. "Bo" Torbert Jr. was an Alabama state senator when elected as chief justice. Jean A. Turnage was a Montana legislator for two decades and served as president of the state senate. His fellow Montanan Mike McGrath was attorney general when he was elected to the judiciary. John L. Hill Jr. of Texas was an active Democratic politician, serving as secretary of state and attorney general before losing the 1978 gubernatorial election (Selby 2007). Jack Holt Jr., elected chief justice in Arkansas, lacked judicial experience but was an attorney of national reputation who served briefly as the state's attorney general and came from a family prominent in state government.[4] Holt's father was a four-term Arkansas attorney general and two-time gubernatorial candidate, and two of their close relatives served as justices in the Arkansas Supreme Court.

From 1970 to 2021, the lone chief justice without judicial experience who was chosen by legislative election was Joseph A. Bevilacqua of Rhode Island. He had been Speaker of the House since 1969 and coordinated his own unanimous election as chief justice in 1976 (United Press International 1986). Bevilacqua faced investigations into his ties to organized

Table 2.1. Chief Justices without Previous Judicial Experience, 1970–2021

State	Chief Justice	Tenure began	Selection method	Immediate prior occupation
Alabama	Howell T. Heflin	1971	Partisan election	Private practice, Alabama Ethics Commission
Alabama	Clement C. Torbert	1977	Partisan election	Private practice, Alabama Senate
Alabama	Drayton Nabers Jr.	2004	Gubernatorial appointment	State finance director
Arkansas	Webster L. Hubbell	1984	Gubernatorial appointment	Private practice, Little Rock City Board of Directors
Arkansas	Jack W. Holt Jr.	1985	Partisan election	Private practice
Arkansas	Bradley D. Jesson	1995	Gubernatorial appointment	Private practice
Arkansas	Betty C. Dickey	2004	Gubernatorial appointment	Chief legal counsel to Governor Mike Huckabee
California	Rose E. Bird	1977	Gubernatorial appointment	California Secretary of Agriculture
Delaware	E. Norman Veasey	1992	Gubernatorial appointment	Private practice
Hawaii	William S. Richardson	1966	Gubernatorial appointment	Lieutenant Governor of Hawaii
Maine	Vincent L. McKusick	1977	Gubernatorial appointment	Private practice
Minnesota	Eric J. Magnuson	2008	Gubernatorial appointment	Private practice, chair of Minnesota Commission on Judicial Selection
Montana	James T. Harrison	1957	Gubernatorial appointment	Malta city attorney and Philips County attorney
Montana	Jean A. Turnage	1985	Nonpartisan election	Montana Senate
Montana	Mike McGrath	2009	Nonpartisan election	Attorney General of Montana
Nebraska	Norman M. Krivosha	1978	Gubernatorial appointment	Private practice
Nebraska	Michael G. Heavican	2006	Gubernatorial appointment	U.S. Attorney, District of Nebraska
New Hampshire	Gordon J. MacDonald	2021	Gubernatorial appointment	Attorney General of New Hampshire
New Jersey	Robert N. Wilentz	1979	Gubernatorial appointment	Private practice

Table 2.1—*Continued*

State	Chief Justice	Tenure began	Selection method	Immediate prior occupation
New Jersey	Deborah T. Poritz	1996	Gubernatorial appointment	Attorney General of New Jersey
New Jersey	Stuart J. Rabner	2007	Gubernatorial appointment	Attorney General of New Jersey
Rhode Island	Joseph A. Bevilacqua	1976	Legislative appointment	Speaker of Rhode Island House of Representatives
Texas	John L. Hill Jr.	1985	Partisan election	Private practice
Vermont	Frederic W. Allen	1984	Gubernatorial appointment	Private practice
Vermont	Jeffrey L. Amestoy	1997	Gubernatorial appointment	Attorney General of Vermont

crime and various felony associates throughout his tenure. He was censured for bringing disrepute to his office in 1985 and resigned while facing impeachment hearings in 1986 (Moakley and Cornwell 2001).

POLITICAL EXPERIENCE

There is a long history of chief justices having experience in the executive or legislative branch. As early as 1777, Thomas McKean of Pennsylvania served as chief justice while he was Speaker of the House and had a brief tenure as acting president (governor) of the young state.[5] While similar violations of the separation of powers have not been normalized, many individuals became court leaders after stints in other branches of government. Just over 14 percent of chief justices in our data had experience as state legislators. A handful of chief justices in this period previously served as governors ($N = 6$) or members of Congress ($N = 3$). Given the multiple roles of chief justice as court leader, liaison to the legislature, and the public face of the court, skills associated with political experience may be beneficial.

In rare instances, legislators have used their positions to orchestrate their own selection as chief justice. Joseph A. Bevilacqua (discussed above) was not the first successful Rhode Island House leader to promote his own bid for chief justice. Edmund W. Flynn was House majority leader before his election to chief justice by the state legislature as part of Rhode Island's "Bloodless Revolution" of 1935. Among other consequences, the historical episode ousted all five members of the state high court. Flynn helped orchestrate the revolutionary events, insisting on appointment as chief justice if he facilitated the Democratic takeover of government via procedural tactics and refusal to seat some Republicans (Bakst 1985). Similar events should be exceedingly rare in the modern era, as all states but South Carolina have abandoned legislative selection of chief justices.

It is feasible that prior service as a legislator can color the reaction to a chief justice facing reappointment. One former legislator turned chief justice, Robert N. Wilentz of New Jersey, narrowly avoided being the first justice on his court to be ousted by the legislature upon reappointment in 1986. Wilentz served two terms in the state legislature as a Democratic representative and had no judicial experience before becoming chief justice. During his tenure, he was known for trying to "streamline the state courts, make them more accessible and use them to promote his vision of social progress and equality." His activism as a court leader was arguably a result of skills honed during his legislative tenure. In addition to a tendency to build intracourt consensus, these skills included "his ability to see political realities and his willingness to push for regulatory and administrative machinery to enforce the court's decrees" (Stout 1996). When he was nominated for reappointment by Republican governor Thomas H. Kean, Wilentz's detractors criticized him for being a liberal judicial activist and spending much of his personal time in Manhattan while his wife received chemotherapy treatments for cancer in New York. Wilentz was reconfirmed narrowly by a vote of 21–19.

Wilentz was not the only chief justice whose leadership style was likely shaped by his legislative experience. A colleague of Montana chief justice Jean A. Turnage observed, "Jean was a politician. He came to the court from the legislature. After having had to work with the numerous individuals in that body, I suspect that his working with just six other justices was pretty much a piece of cake" (Nelson 2015). Justice Sandra Day O'Connor had similar expectations regarding Turnage given his legislative experience, telling an audience of judges and lawyers that Turnage was "uniquely equipped to help" with greater court financing, was "someone with more legislative experience than you would normally find," and knew "the ins and outs" of budgeting.[6]

Chief justices with experience in the U.S. Congress have been rare. Since 1970, just three men served both in Congress and as chief justice. Ernest W. McFarland of Arizona was a two-term U.S senator from 1941 to 1953 and later the state's governor, before he became a justice (and chief justice in 1968). W. Carlton Mobley of Georgia served a single term in the U.S. House in the 1930s before becoming a justice on the state supreme court two decades later. The most recent example of a U.S. House member who became chief justice is Charles T. Canady of Florida. Nearly a decade passed between his stints as a congressman and chief justice, during which he worked for Florida governor Jeb Bush and served as a state appellate judge.

A fourth former congressman, Justice Charles L. Weltner of Georgia, served as a chief justice temporarily in 1992. At the time, Weltner was gravely ill with esophageal cancer. Chief Justice Harold G. Clarke and his colleagues transferred the title to Weltner temporarily to honor him. This allowed Weltner to follow in the footsteps of his great-great-grandfather, Joseph Henry Lumpkin, the first chief justice of Georgia. Weltner became chief justice on June 30, 1992, and participated in his final opinion on July 16. He died in August 1992 and Clarke resumed his position as chief justice (Wannamaker 1999; Weltner 1994).[7]

That all six modern chief justices who served as governors became court leaders before 1984 suggests that this career path has become quite unusual.[8] Like the legislators discussed here, several chief justices who were governors have been described as particularly effective due to skills associated with their earlier leadership of the executive branch. New Jersey Chief Justice Richard J. Hughes, for example, was perceived as a major proponent of judicial reform, and much of his administrative success was attributed to his leadership skills (Sullivan 1977). He was governor from 1962 to 1970 and then appointed as chief justice in 1973.[9] In 1977, Hughes leaned into his experience with interbranch relations when he delivered New Jersey's first State of the Judiciary address to a joint session of the state legislature, the governor, and his judicial colleagues.

Although the political backgrounds of chief justices are more often discussed in terms of their utility for building consensus and navigating interbranch relations, political experience can be detrimental for chief justices if they are perceived as overtly ambitious or jockeying to run for political office. For example, Texas Chief Justice John L. Hill Jr. triggered intracourt conflict when he called for the adoption of merit selection in his 1987 State of the Judiciary address. Soon afterward, a majority of the Texas Supreme Court announced their opposition to his proposal. Justice Oscar H. Mauzy accused Hill of using the issue to promote himself for a 1990 run for governor. Hill had previously served as secretary of state and attorney general and had lost competitive elections for other positions, including the 1978 gubernatorial election.[10] Hill ultimately resigned his seat in 1988 to devote more time to promoting judicial selection reform (Martin 2007).

Certain professional experiences may also be associated with a greater likelihood that an individual will be elevated to the chief justice position. For example, Langer et al. (2003) found that serving as vice chief justice or temporary chief justice increases one's odds of being elected as chief justice by colleagues. It stands to reason that individuals who operate within the court know what is necessary for effective leadership in that structure and would lean toward candidates with prior leadership experience.

Personal Characteristics of Chief Justices

For most of American history, the status of every chief justice in America as a white man was consistent with the overall profile of the bar and bench. Until recent decades, racial minorities and women were largely excluded from the legal profession. While the first African American and female state supreme court justices were elected in 1870 and 1922 respectively, diverse high court judges remained rare for decades.[11] There was not another wave of female or minority judges until a small number of each was appointed from 1959 to 1969 (Goelzhauser 2011, 2016). Not until the 1970s and 1980s did female and minority judges occupy more than a handful of seats on state high courts (Goelzhauser 2011; Hurwitz and Lanier 2003, 2008; Martin and Pyle 2002). The rise of female and minority chief justices followed several years later, as diverse associate justices increased in number and rose in seniority.

FEMALE CHIEF JUSTICES

In a 1994 study of female chief justices, Stockmeyer remarked that "precious few women have risen to the top" of state judiciaries (Stockmeyer 1994, 9). At the time, he reported that only eleven women had done so.[12] Nearly 30 years later, 42 of the 52 state high courts have been led by a woman.[13] In 2020, 21 of the 52 state high courts (40.38 percent) were led by a female chief justice or presiding judge.

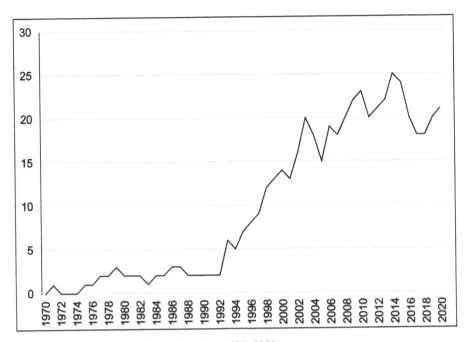

Fig. 2. Number of female chief justices, 1970–2020

The number of female state court leaders from 1970 to 2020 is shown in figure 2. As Stockmeyer indicated in his study, very few women became chief justices prior to the mid-1990s. There was resistance to female chief justices in some states even after women began to reach the judiciary in greater numbers. For example, Charles W. Daniels of New Mexico's high court recounted to a journalist that "there were three justices who were adamant" that Mary Coon Walters "would never be elected chief justice" in the 1980s, even though Walters had been chief judge of the New Mexico Court of Appeals (Weideman 2016). Walters never became chief justice, and four different men held the post during her tenure.[14] However, the number of female court leaders escalated in the last quarter century as the judiciary diversified. By 2014, male and female chief justices were present in nearly equal numbers. Since its peak, the number of female chief justices declined somewhat by 2020, but women in chief justice seats are clearly not unusual in the modern day.

Many female chief justices acknowledge their trailblazing status in public discourse. For example, Georgia Chief Justice Leah Ward Sears explained that being a Black, female jurist came with added pressure.

I have felt both the pressure and the backlash in my career from my status as a "trailblazer." Everyone is watching, especially other young women and even my daughter. But also, there are always naysayers who will call into question your merit and the worthiness of your achievements—I know this for certain from the many campaigns I had to run. You can't worry too much about these people, but for the many that are watching and aspiring to follow behind in my footsteps, I never want anyone to rightfully say these naysayers are speaking the truth. And so, there is tremendous pressure to not mess things up— even if it is only self-imposed. (Timmons-Goodson 2010, 4–5)

Table 2.2 lists pioneering female court leaders prior to 2000. Each of these women became chief justice or chief judge in a period when female court leaders were atypical but gradually becoming more common, exceeding 25 percent of all states by 2000.

The first female chief justice in the United States was Lorna E. Lockwood, who was elected to the Arizona Supreme Court in 1960 and became its chief justice in 1965. Lockwood was selected as chief justice by a vote of her peers on two occasions, serving in that capacity from 1965 to 1966 and in 1970. Lockwood was the daughter of Alfred C. Lockwood, who also served as chief justice during his 17 years on the Arizona Supreme Court (1925–42). Lorna Lockwood was the only woman in her law class at the University of Arizona and faced considerable difficulty establishing a legal career. She was elected as a state legislator in 1939 and then held several offices in state government before joining the state's high court.

Lockwood was the only female chief justice in American history until Susie Marshall Sharp of North Carolina became the first selected by voters in 1974. Sharp was appointed as an associate justice in 1962 without the backing of the court's outgoing chief justice, J. Wallace Winborne. North Carolina governor J. Terry Sanford privately solicited Winborne's opinion about the possibility of appointing Sharp, and Winborne was not supportive, saying, "Governor, the supreme court is a man's court" (Hayes 2008, 232). Nonetheless, Sanford appointed Sharp. She was the senior associate justice when she ran for chief justice in 1974. The incumbent chief, William H. Bobbitt, faced mandatory retirement due to age but declined to retire early because he did not want the state's Republican governor to appoint his successor. Sharp won 74 percent of the statewide vote, defeating a Republican opponent who lacked a law degree (Hayes 2008).

Table 2.2. Female Chief Justices, 1965–99

Years	Chief Justice	State	Selection method
1965–66, 1971	Lorna E. Lockwood	Arizona	Peer vote
1975–79	Susie Marshall Sharp	North Carolina	Partisan election
1977–87	Rose E. Bird[a]	California	Appointed by governor
1979–82	Mary Stallings Coleman	Michigan	Peer vote
1984–96	Ellen Ash Peters	Connecticut	Appointed by governor
1986	Rhoda S. Billings[b]	North Carolina	Appointed by governor
1987–91	Dorothy Comstock Riley	Michigan	Peer vote
1992–94	Rosemary Barkett	Florida	Peer vote
1993, 1997, 2011, 2015, 2018	Margaret L. Workman	West Virginia	Peer vote
1993–95	Ann K. Covington	Missouri	Peer vote
1993–2008	Judith S. Kaye	New York	Appointed by governor
1995–97	Alma Bell Wilson	Oklahoma	Peer vote
1995–98	Barbara M. Durham	Washington	Peer vote
1995–2009	Kay E. McFarland	Kansas	Seniority
1996–2006	Deborah T. Poritz	New Jersey	Appointed by governor
1996–2015	Shirley S. Abrahamson	Wisconsin	Seniority
1997, 2004	Miriam M. Shearing	Nevada	Rotation by seniority
1997–2004	Linda Copple Trout	Idaho	Peer vote
1998–2001	Lenore L. Prather	Mississippi	Seniority
1998–2006	Kathleen A. Blatz	Minnesota	Appointed by governor
1998–2010	Mary J. Mullarkey	Colorado	Peer vote
1999–2010	Margaret H. Marshall	Massachusetts	Appointed by governor

Source: Stockmeyer (1994), Goelzhauser (2016), and court websites.

[a] Bird lost a reelection bid in 1986.

[b] Billings received her commission in September 1986 but was defeated in the November election of that year by Associate Justice James G. Exum Jr.

During Sharp's tenure as chief justice, female court leaders also took office in California and Michigan. Rose E. Bird was serving on the cabinet of California governor Jerry Brown when she was appointed to the center seat in 1977. She had no previous judicial experience. Her tenure was tumultuous, with conservative activists working for her ouster almost from the start (Hood 1978, A1). Her opponents successfully roused public outrage about her court's perceived leniency in decisions involving the death penalty, leading to the electoral defeat of Bird and two other (male) Brown appointees in 1986 (Egelko 1986). Mary S. Coleman was elected as Michigan chief justice by her fellow justices and held the position from 1979 until her retirement in 1982. Coleman's tenure was more conventional than Bird's, and she dedicated herself to major administrative reforms, reorganizing Wayne County's court system, revising Michigan's juvenile justice and probate codes, and securing state funding for courts (Associated Press 2001).

Just three women became chief justices during the 1980s, but women chief justices were less unusual by the 1990s and 2000s. Some women were among the most influential state chief justices in the modern era (e.g., Judith S. Kaye and Jean Hoefer Toal), went on to the federal appellate courts (e.g., Rosemary Barkett), or were considered as potential U.S. Supreme Court justices (e.g., Shirley S. Abrahamson, Judith S. Kaye, and Leah Ward Sears). Others were famously involved in intracourt and interbranch feuds (e.g., Shirley S. Abrahamson) or were defeated in high-profile elections (e.g., Rose E. Bird and Marsha K. Ternus).

The growing number of female chief justices has allowed the examination of patterns in their leadership. For example, some political scientists argue that female court leaders are skilled consensus builders (Leonard and Ross 2020). Other scholars conclude that female court leaders are more focused on amicable relations with legislators (Norris 2022). When social scientists have examined the administrative leadership of female chief justices, they have not identified significant differences in the success rates of male and female chiefs (Wilhelm, Vining, Boldt, and Black 2020). Given the regular elevation of women as chief justices in the modern era, it is evident that scholars will have many more opportunities to analyze the impact of gender on court leadership.

NONWHITE MINORITIES AS CHIEF JUSTICES

People of color have always been underrepresented among the memberships of state high courts (Acquaviva and Castiglione 2009; Goelzhauser 2011; Martin and Pyle 2002). Members of minority groups were excluded systematically from the legal profession and law schools for much of American history. That exclusion had obvious consequences for their participation in the judiciary. While there were unusual exceptions such as Jonathan Jasper Wright, the aforementioned South Carolina justice during Reconstruction, racial diversity on state supreme courts did not

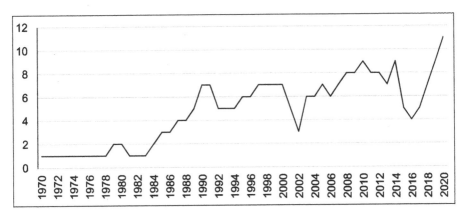

Fig. 3. Number of minority chief justices, 1970–2020

begin to increase substantially until the mid-1970s (Acquaviva and Castiglione 2009; Goelzhauser 2011). Before that decade, state high court judges from minority racial groups were rare, and very few nonwhite individuals became chief justices. In figure 3, we display the number of minority chief justices in the states over time. The quantity of minority chiefs has been relatively small throughout American history, but the annual total recently reached double digits.

From 1970 until 1983, there were only three nonwhite chief justices in America (Dan Sosa Jr. of New Mexico and William S. Richardson and Herman T. F. Lum of Hawaii). The number of minority chief justices exceeded a half dozen in 1990, when the ranks of those court leaders included two Black men (Robert N. C. Nix Jr. of Pennsylvania and Leander J. Shaw Jr. of Florida), three Hispanic individuals (Dorothy Comstock Riley of Michigan, Luis D. Rovira of Colorado, and Dan Sosa Jr. of New Mexico), a Chinese American man (Herman T. F. Lum of Hawaii), and a Native American man (Jean A. Turnage of Montana). By 2002, only three nonwhite chief justices remained in office. By 2020, eleven court leaders (six men and five women) were from minority racial backgrounds.

From 1970 to 2020, 21 states had a chief justice from a minority racial group (see table 2.3). Overall, 24 of those 39 chief justices were African American, with the majority of those 24 serving in former Confederate or border states. The first wave of Southern Black chief justices occurred in the 1990s in Florida, South Carolina, Georgia, Maryland, and North Carolina. Georgia Chief Justice Robert Benham explained that Black chief justices in states once subject to slavery and racial segregation were

Table 2.3. States with Minority Chief Justices, 1970–2020

African American	Hispanic American	Asian American	Native American
Connecticut (1)	Colorado (1)	California (1)	Montana (1)
Florida (2)	Florida (1)	Hawaii (3)	
Georgia (3)	Michigan (1)	New Mexico (1)	
Illinois (1)	New Mexico (3)		
Louisiana (1)	Oregon (1)		
Maryland (1)			
Massachusetts (2)			
Michigan (2)			
Missouri (2)			
North Carolina (2)			
Oklahoma (1)			
Pennsylvania (1)			
South Carolina (2)			
Texas (1)			
Virginia (1)			

Note: The number of minority chief justices for each state are shown in parentheses.

symbolic of the progress made in American society: "No one would have believed that a grandchild of a slave would end up being chief justice of that same court that had once ignored what they were experiencing" (Chappell 1997). Georgia Chief Justice Leah Ward Sears expressed similar sentiments, noting that her father and people of his generation were affected greatly by her appointment.

> He was shocked at the opportunity that was breaking forth for his daughter. I think, racially, he was surprised. He would really be floored that Barack Obama was elected president. But he would have been equally floored at the progress of this state, not because of my qualifications, but because the people of this state could accept somebody like me as their chief justice. (Sears 2009, E1)

The nine Hispanic American chief justices since 1970 are from a relatively diverse geographic area, but six were grouped in western states with historically large Hispanic/Latino populations (Colorado and New Mexico). Florida chief justice Jorge Labarga was a Cuban American who migrated to the state as a young boy. His immigration story is relatable to many individuals in Florida's large and politically significant Cuban American population.

The Asian American chief justices since 1970 are primarily rooted in Hawaii and California, both of which have substantial populations of

Asian ancestry. The lone Native American serving as state chief justice hailed from Montana, one of several western states with sizable populations of indigenous peoples.

Table 2.4 lists the nonwhite minorities among state court leaders through 2020. The earliest nonwhite chief justices we identified predate the 1970 threshold used in the descriptive statistics given above. Our research of court histories and judicial biographies indicates that Eugene D. Lujan of New Mexico was the first Hispanic chief justice. He became the court's leader via rotation by seniority and served two stints as chief in the 1950s. He was followed by David Chavez Jr. of New Mexico in 1967. Two Asian American chief justices, Wilfred C. Tsukiyama and William S. Richardson, led Hawaii's high court from statehood until the early 1980s. The earliest Black chief justice was Robert N. C. Nix Jr. of Pennsylvania, who became chief by seniority in 1984. The only member of a Native American tribe to serve as chief justice was Jean A. Turnage of Montana, who led his court from 1985 to 2000. Notably, Turnage is the only individual from the list in table 2.4 who became chief via popular election. The earliest female minority court leader was Dorothy Comstock Riley of Michigan, whose mother was Mexican.[15] In 2005, Leah Ward Sears of Georgia was the first Black woman to become chief justice.

On a related note, the first openly LGBTQ chief justice of a state, C. Shannon Bacon of New Mexico, took office in April 2022 after being elected as chief by her colleagues (Bacon 2023). In addition, the New York Court of Appeals selected gay judge Anthony Cannataro as its acting chief judge in August 2022 after the resignation of Chief Judge Janet M. DiFiore (Gavin 2022). Another gay justice, Andrew J. McDonald of Connecticut, was nominated for elevation to chief in 2018. However, he was not confirmed. McDonald was nominated by a Democratic governor and lacked support from Republicans in the state legislature who criticized him as a liberal partisan and judicial activist. His nomination was approved 75–74 in the House but defeated by a 19–16 vote in the Senate (Dixon 2018).

Research on the Selection of Diverse Chief Justices

There is little empirical research about the selection of female or minority chief justices. Political scientists and other researchers frequently focus on judicial selection and tenure in the states, but they seldom turn their attention specifically to court leaders. Since our focus here is diversity in the ranks of judicial leadership, we review and extend research that examines the proliferation of nontraditional chiefs.

Table 2.4. Nonwhite Minority Chief Justices, 1951–2020

Years	Chief Justice	Background	State	Selection method
1951–52, 1957–59	Eugene D. Lujan	Hispanic	NM	Rotation by seniority
1959–65	Wilfred C. Tsukiyama	Asian American	HI	Appointed by governor
1966–82	William S. Richardson	Asian American / Native Hawaiian / Caucasian	HI	Appointed by governor
1967–68	David Chavez Jr.	Hispanic	NM	Peer vote
1979–80, 1989–91	Daniel Sosa Jr.	Hispanic	NM	Peer vote
1982–93	Herman T. F. Lum	Asian American	HI	Appointed by governor
1984–96	Robert N. C. Nix Jr.	African American	PA	Seniority
1985–2000	Jean A. Turnage	Native American	MT	Nonpartisan election
1987–91	Dorothy Comstock Riley	Hispanic	MI	Peer vote
1990–92	Leander J. Shaw Jr.	African American	FL	Peer vote
1990–95	Luis D. Rovira	Hispanic	CO	Peer vote
1992–94	Rosemary Barkett	Syrian American	FL	Peer vote
1993–2010	Ronald T. Y. Moon	Asian American	HI	Appointed by governor
1994–2000	Ernest A. Finney Jr.	African American	SC	Elected by legislature
1995–2001	Robert Benham	African American	GA	Peer vote
1996–2013	Robert M. Bell	African American	MD	Appointed by governor
1997–98	Conrad L. Mallett Jr.	African American	MI	Peer vote
1997–99	Charles E. Freeman	African American	IL	Peer vote
1999–2001	Henry E. Frye	African American	NC	Appointed by governor
2001–3	Patricio M. Serna	Hispanic	NM	Peer vote
2003–5	Ronnie L. White	African American	MO	Peer vote
2003–5, 2012–14	Petra Jimenez Maes	Hispanic	NM	Peer vote
2003–11	Leroy R. Hassell Sr.	African American	VA	Peer vote
2004–13	Wallace B. Jefferson	African American	TX	Appointed by governor
2005–9	Leah Ward Sears	African American	GA	Peer vote
2006–12	Paul J. De Muniz	Hispanic	OR	Peer vote
2007–10	Edward L. Chavez	Hispanic	NM	Peer vote
2008–10	Peggy A. Quince	African American	FL	Peer vote
2010–14	Roderick L. Ireland	African American	MA	Appointed by governor
2011–17	Robert P. Young Jr.	African American	MI	Peer vote

Table 2.4—*Continued*

Years	Chief Justice	Background	State	Selection method
2011-22	Tani G. Cantil-Sakauye	Asian American	CA	Appointed by governor
2013–14, 2019–21	David B. Lewis	African American	OK (CCA)	Peer vote
2013–15	Thomas Colbert	African American	OK	Peer vote
2013–20	Bernette Joshua Johnson	African American	LA	Seniority
2014–18	Jorge Labarga	Hispanic	FL	Peer vote
2017–present	Donald W. Beatty	African American	SC	Elected by legislature
2017–20	Judith K. Nakamura	Asian American	NM	Peer vote
2018–21	Harold D. Melton	African American	GA	Peer vote
2018–present	Richard A. Robinson	African American	CT	Appointed by governor
2019–20	Cheri L. Beasley	African American	NC	Appointed by governor
2019–21	George W. Draper III	African American	MO	Peer vote
2020-22	Michael E. Vigil	Hispanic	NM	Peer vote
2020–present	Kimberly S. Budd	African American	MA	Appointed by governor

PREVIOUS RESEARCH

Scholars have reported some general findings about the institutional and political factors associated with women's ascension to judicial leadership positions. In a time-structured analysis, Norris and Tankersley (2018) examined peer votes for chief justices between 1970 and 2008. Their findings indicate that state supreme court justices are more likely to choose women as their leaders when the court is ideologically diverse, when the supply of experienced women on the court is greater, and when chief justices serve longer terms.

Similar inquiries on the timing and selection of minority chief justices do not exist. The closest analogues examine minority representation on courts generally (Alozie 1988, 1990; B. L. Graham 1990) or on state supreme courts. Most instructive is research by Goelzhauser (2011, 2016) that examines the relationship between selection systems and overall diversity on state supreme courts from 1960 to 2014. He found that the probability of seating minority justices was lower in election systems than in systems using merit or government appointment. He also found that diverse justices (both women and racial or ethnic minorities) were

Table 2.5. Percentages of Women and Minorities Holding Seats on State Supreme Courts

	Chief Justices (1970–2020)	All Seats (1960–2014)
Women	15%	16%
Minorities	7%	9%
Total diverse chiefs	20%	23%

Source: Data for the column "All Seats" is from Goelzhauser 2016.

more likely to be seated in states where high court judges are appointed.

There are obvious limitations to the existing body of research, particularly as it pertains to the selection of minority chief justices. We know what factors are associated with the selection of female chief justices where peer voting is used, but we do not have the same framework for understanding the rise of women in other systems of chief justice selection. As far as understanding minority leadership on state supreme courts, we know very little. Our analysis of factors associated with the selection of diverse chief justices follows.

RESEARCH UPDATE

To improve our understanding of the factors associated with the selection of diverse court leaders, we use data on all chief justices who served in state supreme courts between 1970 and 2020 (the same data described in chapter 1). Of the 541 chief justices in that period, 80 (14.79 percent) were women, and 39 (7.20 percent) were nonwhite minorities. Represented in these data are a total of 109 nontraditional justices (20.15 percent of the total). Interestingly, these percentages are similar to diversity trends for all state supreme court seats (see table 2.5).

Between 1960 and 2014, 16 percent of all state supreme court seats were filled by women, 9 percent by nonwhite minorities, and 23 percent by diverse judges overall (Goelzhauser 2016, 102). The similar levels of female and nonwhite representation among chief justices and associate justices support conclusions drawn by Norris and Tankersley (2018) regarding the impact of a larger pool of nontraditional candidates. They determine that diversity among high court judges yields diversity among court leaders. While their study focused on chiefs elected via peer vote, selection systems rooted in seniority or rotation also should produce

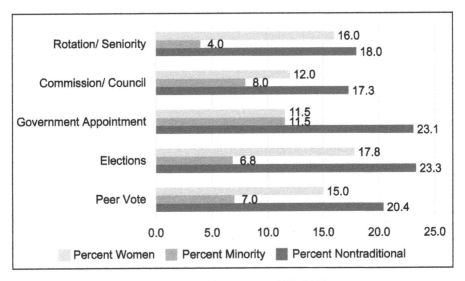

Fig. 4. Percentages of nontraditional chief justices, 1970–2020

diverse chiefs as women and minorities gain a foothold in the judiciary. Popular elections and appointment systems, however, are more likely to depend on elite preferences or statewide political conditions.

Figure 4 provides a preliminary view of the diversity of chief justices within each selection system. Relative to men, women have been selected as chief justices most frequently in election systems (17.8 percent) and picked for the lowest proportion of chief justiceships in systems of government appointment (11.5 percent). Interestingly, relative to white chiefs, minority chief justices are more common in systems of government appointment than in alternative selection schemes (11.5 percent). Minorities have held the lowest proportion of seats in rotation/seniority systems (4.0 percent). Overall, nontraditional chief justices make up a relatively consistent percentage of chief justice seats across all types of selection systems (from 17.3 to 23.3 percent).

Further investigation is important to determine whether any selection system is more likely to produce female or nonwhite chief justices. We analyzed each state selection of a chief justice between 1970 and 2020 to ascertain how selection systems relate to the elevation of nontraditional chiefs (data for selection events are described in chapter 1). Our statistical model estimates the likelihood that a selected chief justice was (1) female, (2) a minority, or (3) diverse (female and/or a minority).

Table 2.6. Selection Methods and Female, Minority, and Diverse Chief Justices, 1970–2020

	Female Chief Justices	Minority Chief Justices	Diverse Chief Justices
Peer vote	0.18	1.39	**0.76***
	(0.29)	(0.94)	**(0.41)**
Election	0.21	0.83	0.52
	(−0.41)	(1.10)	(0.55)
Government appoint- ment (without commission)	−0.29	1.45	0.51
	(0.35)	(1.00)	(0.49)
Commission	−0.49	1.01	0.21
	(0.48)	(1.02)	(0.52)
Rotation/seniority	*omitted*	*omitted*	*omitted*
Citizen ideology (liberalism)	**0.02***	**0.02***	**0.02****
	(0.01)	**(.01)**	**(0.01)**
Court size	**0.15***	0.03	0.13
	(0.07)	(0.20)	(0.12)
Mandatory retirement	0.20	0.17	0.12
	(0.19)	(0.55)	(0.28)
Constant	−3.63**	−4.73*	−4.02*
	(0.59)	(1.52)	(1.04)

We used data provided by Goelzhauser (2016) updated through 2020 to measure our dependent variables.

We also analyzed the impact of several control variables, like those included in Goelzhauser's (2016) analysis of diversity in state supreme court seats. Our variables include court size, mandatory retirement rules, and state citizen ideology.[16] Data on court size and retirement rules were obtained from state court websites and *The Book of the States* (Council of State Governments 2020). Citizen ideology data were obtained from Berry, et al. (2013).

Given that each dependent variable is dichotomous, the models are fit with logistic regression. Standard errors are clustered by state to account for nonindependence within states. The results of our models are reported in table 2.6. While the estimated coefficients and standard errors provide important information, the substantive impacts of the variables are not readily interpretable. The discussion and figures that follow provide the results of postestimation techniques that indicate changes in predicted probabilities related to variables of significance. We also provide the 95 percent confidence intervals around the predicted change in probability.

Our analysis reveals that no selection system is more likely to pro-

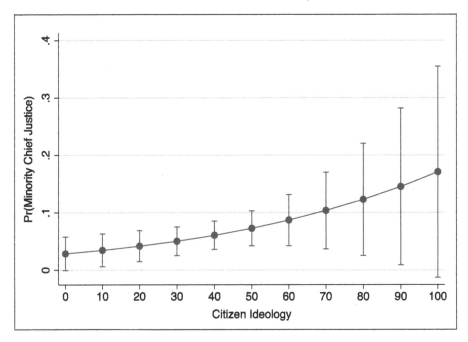

Fig. 5. Predicted probability of selecting a nontraditional chief justice, across citizen ideology

duce women or minority chiefs when we consider those categories separately. However, we find that diverse chief justices (aggregated) are more likely to be chosen where peer votes are used to select court leaders. In our postestimation results, the average predicted probability of diverse selection is 14.4 percent, which increases to 24.7 percent in peer vote systems. That finding suggests that women and minorities have greater odds of becoming chief justices where their colleagues promote from within, though neither subset of justices is favored versus the other. Given that many peer vote norms tend to recognize seniority, that result is sensible as women and nonwhites reach high courts more often and serve longer tenures.

While selection systems overall have a limited impact on the proliferation of women or minority chief justices, citizen ideology is significant and positive in all three models. The results demonstrate, undoubtedly, that states with more liberal citizens have an increased likelihood of having women and/or minority chief justices. In substantive terms, our postestimation results reveal that the most conservative state would have a 4 percent likelihood of selecting a nontraditional chief justice, while the most liberal state would have a 48 percent likelihood of selecting a nontraditional chief justice. No state population skews so completely left or right, but the range is still informative. The graphed results for our model of the impact of citizen ideology on selection of a nontraditional chief justice is shown in figure 5. For the diversity of individuals who will serve as chief justice, the political environment within a state has more influence than the structure of the chief justice institution.

Conclusion

Analysis of the professional experiences and personal characteristics of the state chief justices provides an informative overview of the individuals who serve in those positions. In terms of their backgrounds, we find that most individuals have judicial experience before they serve as chief justice or chief judge, an expected finding even for systems where chiefs need not come from the high court's roster. Court leaders without judicial experience tend to benefit from popular elections or appointment systems. The prevalence of other legal and political experiences that individuals had before becoming chief justice is notable, with more variety than one might expect. For example, it is not intuitive that approximately one in every seven chiefs served as state legislator or that several governors would shift to chief justiceships later in their careers. We posit that prior professional experience affects how chief justices navigate the political environments of their states.

Our research also reveals that state chief justices have been a more diverse lot than their federal counterparts. Women make up a significant proportion of chief justice seats in the modern era, while minority representation among state chief justices has grown less rapidly. Our analysis of systems of chief justice selection reveals that states assigning that responsibility to the high court are more likely to seat diverse chief justices, but state liberalism is the best predictor for whether diverse chiefs will lead a state's high court.

Our findings motivate several interesting questions. What can we learn from states that have selected chief justices with no judicial experience? That those individuals were all chosen through government appointment or by popular election suggests that, where the selection method allows, prospective court leaders who are ambitious or have a powerful benefactor can sidestep the norm of judicial experience. Interestingly, several of these individuals gained reputations as capable judicial administrators after joining the bench. In some instances, this success was attributed to familiarity with the policymaking process the justices had to navigate as advocates for the judiciary.

Second, given the growing number of female chief justices, why have 8 states not yet named a female chief justice? A third, similar query is relevant for the 29 states where no nonwhite chief justice has served. Those questions are important well beyond keeping score. Political scientists have found that greater diversity on courts is associated with increased legitimacy for the judiciary, particularly among historically under-represented groups (Kenney 2012; Redman 2021; Scherer and Curry 2010). On a more practical note, Illinois Chief Justice Charles Freeman explained that diversity on his court fostered a better understanding of issues on its docket.

> When people of different backgrounds and different persuasions can sit down and express views privately to other judges and make points that they [others] may not understand, diversity ends up being good for understanding some of the issues before us and some of the social problems that are created in those issues.[17]

We suggest these issues are particularly relevant at a time when Americans increasingly recognize the historical biases that affect political institutions, their composition, and their outputs.

PART 2

CHAPTER 3

The Chief Justice as Administrator

Mary J. Mullarkey was a trailblazer in Colorado politics. She was the first female chief justice and the longest serving court leader in the state's history. In a reflective 2021 interview with *Colorado Politics*, Mullarkey revealed that her most memorable accomplishment from her 12-year tenure as chief justice was not among the 472 court opinions she authored. The crowning achievement she recounted was an administrative feat that took considerable extrajudicial effort.

> One of my big achievements was to get the new court building [Carr Center], and it took 10 years for me to get that done. And I think that in terms of getting it funded and done, getting it paid for—from what I remember of the old building, there were really a lot of problems with the building. I wrote to the legislators and invited them to come around so I could show them all the problems we were having with the building. It's funny because they were nodding their heads and saying, "Oh, yes, we agree." And they said, "How are you going to pay for that?"
>
> And it's like: it's the legislature's job to come up with the money and a way to do that!
>
> That sort of issue—how to build a coalition to get the building constructed—that is not something that you could do in two years.

Mullarkey went on to say that she viewed her role as an administrator as central to court leadership.

CP: As the chief justice, you are an administrator and policy-setter in addition to being a vote in cases. What sticks with you more: your accomplishments as the judicial branch's leader, like spearheading the building of the Carr Center, or the cases that you participated in that shaped the legal terrain in Colorado?

MULLARKEY: The administrative things are more important. It was a chance to build that building . . . [but] both are important. It's hard to say. (Karlik 2021)

The new court building—the Ralph L. Carr Colorado Judicial Center— was indeed noteworthy. At 60,000 square feet, it currently houses the Supreme Court, Court of Appeals, and office of the Attorney General for the state of Colorado.

Mullarkey is not the only chief justice to be remembered primarily for infrastructure improvements rather than for influential legal work. In 2018, Louisiana lawmakers passed legislation to name the Chief Justice Pascal F. Calogero, Jr. Courthouse after the long-tenured jurist who spent decades working to revitalize the building. His efforts to restore the courthouse are his most cited achievement, as local news coverage of the naming ceremony confirms.

In 2004, after 20 years of planning, budgetary pitfalls, intermittent support, and countless trips to the Capital to appeal for legislative appropriations, Calogero's vision became reality when the Louisiana Supreme Court moved from its courthouse on Loyola Avenue back to the newly renovated building, where it originally sat from 1910– 1958. . . .

While on the bench, Chief Justice Calogero authored over 1,000 learned majority opinions, concurrences, and dissents. He participated in over 6,000 oral arguments and published opinions. . . . Though he is respected for these accomplishments, he will forever be remembered for his passion and drive to restore and return the Court to its previous location.[1]

Personal recollections of former chief justices and media coverage of judicial leaders often emphasize their administrative accomplishments. Career retrospectives and tributes to chief justices' careers overwhelmingly describe their administrative work above most everything else. These tributes are frequently authored by colleagues or members of the legal community who are well equipped to evaluate the chiefs' leadership efforts. Such accounts stand in contrast to how social scientists tend to view the nature of chief justice leadership (e.g., Gray and Miller 2021). Scholars usually evaluate chief justices with the perspective that their primary functions are tied to case outcomes and legal opinions. It seems strange that chief justices who presided over a Colorado property rights controversy dating back to Mexican territorial rule (*Lobato v. Taylor*, 71 P.3d 938 [2002]) or who ruled against Louisiana's antiquated sodomy laws (*State v. Mitchell Smith*, 99-KA-0606 [2000], dissenting) would be remembered predominantly for administrative actions rather than legal contributions. Yet the anecdotes speak for themselves.

Beyond the career recollections of associates, colleagues, and media, chief justices themselves often underscore their administrative roles. Consider comments by Paul M. Newby of North Carolina, who won election to that state's chief justice position in 2020 after 15 years as associate justice. During the election campaign, he gave a telling answer to a question in Ballotpedia's *Candidate Connection*.

> *Are there any little-known powers or responsibilities held by this office that you believe more people should be aware of?*
>
> The NC Chief Justice is the first among equals of the seven-member NC Supreme Court. In that role, the Chief Justice has additional administrative responsibilities but also decides cases and writes opinions just like the other six justices. The Chief Justice also serves as the leader of the Judicial Branch which is comprised of about 6,500 people across NC. Many who compose the Judicial Branch are independent constitutional officers, including judges and clerks. Thus, the role of Chief Justice is to inspire members of the branch to ensure that every person who interacts with the judicial system receives equal justice under the law.[2]

As Chief Justice Newby reminds us, the administrative nature of chief justice leadership is consequential and should be more widely recognized by scholars interested in courts and interbranch relations. This chapter addresses that aspect of chief justice leadership. We maintain that the states' chief justices are better understood in the modern era as important administrative leaders as well as participants in high court jurisprudence. While serving as "first among equals," a chief justice also has important roles in judicial branch leadership that are not generally shared by colleagues (Raftery 2017; Shepard 2009a). This overtly administrative work, as consequential as intracourt leadership, is perhaps even more significant where courts or judges have been neglected by legislators.

Empowering Chief Justices as Judicial Leaders

In the modern era, state chief justices are responsible for administrative leadership of the judicial branch (Raftery 2017), typically in partnership with professional court administrators, their fellow justices on the state supreme court, and/or a judicial council. The source of this authority is (entirely or partially) the state constitution in 43 states and statutory law in the remaining (Rottman and Strickland 2006, 63–64). This conception of the chief justice position is relatively contemporary. While court leaders have long held some administrative responsibilities in the state judiciary, a notable shift in the significance and capacity of their work occurred since the middle of the 20th century. After a sporadic reform movement lasting more than 50 years, many administrative obligations have been given to chief justices. The gradual shift to empower chief justices was intentional and strategic, as state courts and their allies looked to overcome delays in case processing, fragmented organization, legislative interference, and public suspicion.[3]

The consolidation of court administration to state chief justices and state supreme courts was a central plank of the court unification movement (Hays 1993, 223; Raftery 2013, 342). The judicial branch had long been criticized for inefficient operations and fractured management (Pound 1906). Individual judges traditionally had substantial autonomy, with minimal oversight from administrative authorities to ensure efficiency or equity in their courtrooms. Efforts to consolidate judicial administration or enlist professional administrators to aid the courts began to emerge early in the 20th century. A 1909 special committee of the American Bar Association advocated for a "high official" to supervise the judiciary, and the leadership of the American Judicature Society in 1917 argued that the chief justice should have such authority (Raftery 2013). Prominent reformers including Roscoe Pound (1940), William Willoughby (1929), and Arthur Vanderbilt (1949) also called for unifying administrative authority in the judiciary to promote efficiency and improve interbranch communications. Willoughby (1929, 339) argued that "making provision for a unity of command" was the "most important step" toward improving court administration, with states' chief justices "given the responsibility and powers of a general manager in respect to the whole judicial system." These ideas were not embraced universally or quickly by courts or legislators. However, vigorous advocates such as Pound and Vanderbilt continued to push for a consolidation of judicial administration authority that would empower chief justices and court administrators.

Constitutional provisions and ordinary legislation gradually expanded administrative duties for chief justices throughout the United States, largely achieving a goal long held by boosters of court unification. The bulk of the reforms to consolidate authority in chief justices occurred in the 1960s and 1970s. Raftery (2013) found that 33 states designated the chief justice as the administrative leader of the judicial branch between 1959 and 1978—either alone or as the leader of the state high court. Many of the consolidating reforms were in response to ongoing calls by judges and the legal profession to unify, professionalize, and standardize the operations of state court systems.

The trend toward empowering chief justices was reflected in the American Bar Association's 1974 *Standards Relating to Court Organization*, which explicitly identified chief justices as chief administrative officers of their courts and tasked them with the development of policy agendas (Hays and Douglas 2006, 1004–5). Rather than a "boss in the classical sense," the chief justice would be "a facilitator and coordinator" uniting the judiciary and advancing its goals (Hays and Douglas 2006, 1005). By 1977, Berkson reported, "Every major study since 1942 has advocated placing administrative responsibility for the court system in the chief justice, and nearly all have called for the establishment of a court administrator's office to aid him in this endeavor" (Berkson 1977, 378). Chief justices were often granted substantial administrative authority even where court unification was not achieved in the form imagined by its proponents. Further, the de jure leadership roles of chief justices have enhanced their roles as the de facto public faces of their court systems.

State chief justices began to be recognized as leaders of the judicial branch even before the formal delegation of administrative authority to chiefs and state high courts. More than 50 years ago, Glick (1970, 278) explained that state chief justices had the responsibility to "act as the major spokesmen for the courts in making policy suggestions." At that time, communications from chief justices would have been irregular and informal in most states, with written opinions, personal conferences, and haphazard contacts by individual courts being more common methods of communication between courts and legislators (Glick 1970, 276–82). Nonetheless, the chief justice remained the "titular head of the court, chief administrative officer, and representative to outside groups" and was expected to be "better informed" regarding the judiciary than his colleagues (Ducat and Flango 1976).

The shift toward chief justices as empowered judicial administrators has implications for how we conceive both judicial leadership and the significance of the different kinds of functions in which those leaders serve. In a 2017 study, Raftery refers to chief justices as "court leaders" who lead the state supreme court, "judicial leaders" who oversee and protect the judicial branch, and "justice leaders" who advance values such as fairness and access to justice. The second and third of those roles go well beyond Danelski's classic characterization of chief justices as "task leaders" and "social leaders" on their courts (Danelski 1960; Danelski and Ward 2016). It is up to individual chief justices to decide how much they want to prioritize each of these leadership opportunities, according to their own goals. That many chief justices give highest priority to their role as judicial leaders is indicated by comparing the time and energy they spend in administrative endeavors versus all others (Smith and Feldman 2001).

Facets of Modern Judicial Administrative Leadership

Because the modern chief justice is empowered to be the administrative leader of the state judiciary, the associated duties can be time consuming and onerous. Petra Jimenez Maes of New Mexico remarked in 2003 that her chief justice position required time and activities beyond those of her court colleagues. As she explained, "being chief justice adds 20 hours to your workload just with all the extra administrative duties," and "it's the sort of role where you're the person everyone goes to" (Krueger 2003). Her observations seem to be generalizable. Survey research by Smith and Feldman (2001) found that some chief justices spend as much as 80 percent of their work time on administrative tasks. The same researchers found that associate justices reported spending no more than 20 percent of their time on administrative tasks, often much less.[4]

Even while conceding substantial variation among the states, Tobin argues that there are typically six generic components of a chief justice's administrative leadership: (1) goal setting and leadership; (2) formulation and implementation of management policy; (3) dealing with judges; (4) relationships with the bar; (5) relations with the other branches, noncourt agencies, and the public; and (6) delegation and oversight of the detailed aspects of court administration (Tobin 1999, 149). He points out that "a chief justice is the official spokesperson for the judiciary in both ceremonial matters and in businesslike contacts with the various governmental bodies with which the judiciary interacts" (152). Tobin's list of categories captures the broad scope of judicial administrative leadership. Scholars have observed that chief justices take on leadership responsibilities even where they are not required to do so by legal mandates (Dosal, McQueen, and Wheeler 2007).

FORMAL ADMINISTRATIVE RESPONSIBILITIES

With chief justices spending so much time on administrative tasks, why have scholars largely overlooked that facet of judicial leadership? One reason is the lack of information about these duties. Scholars have outlined the intracourt tasks assigned to states' court leaders (M.G. Hall 1990; Hughes, Wilhelm, and Vining 2015; McConkie 1974, 1976), but less attention has gone to the leaders' extrajudicial duties. The full breadth of chief justice administrative duties across the states has not been cataloged.

A variety of formal administrative responsibilities are assigned to chief justices. In some states, these duties are derived from a formal statutory or constitutional charge that gives only an outline for the leadership responsibilities of the chief justice. For instance, section 51.1b of the Connecticut General Statutes prescribes the job broadly: "(a) The Chief Justice of the Supreme Court shall be the head of the Judicial Department and shall be responsible for its administration."[5] The directive given by the Georgia Constitution is more limited, designating the chief justice only as "the chief presiding and administrative officer of the court."[6] However, the state's chief justice serves as the chair of the Judicial Council of Georgia tasked with policy development and improvements to court administration. Of course, statutory or constitutional text regarding chief justices is not always so slight. For example, Alabama law includes more than 800 words devoted to the duties of the chief justice.[7]

Detailed guidelines regarding the formal parameters of chief justice duties are frequently established by the judicial branch or state high court. For example, the charge to the chief justice in the Florida Rules of Judicial Administration is quite specific.

(B) The chief justice shall be the administrative officer of the judicial branch and of the supreme court and shall be responsible for the dispatch of the business of the branch and of the court and direct the implementation of policies and priorities as determined by the supreme court for the operation of the branch and of the court. The administrative powers and duties of the chief justice shall include, but not be limited to:

(i) the responsibility to serve as the primary spokesperson for the judicial branch regarding policies and practices that have statewide impact including, but not limited to, the judicial branch's management, operation, strategic plan, legislative agenda and budget priorities;

(ii) the power to act on requests for stays during the pendency of proceedings, to order the consolidation of cases, to determine all procedural motions and petitions relating to the time for filing and size of briefs and other papers provided for under the rules of this court, to advance or continue cases, and to rule on other procedural matters relating to any proceeding or process in the court;

(iii) the power to assign active or retired county, circuit, or appellate judges or justices to judicial service in this state, in accordance with subdivisions (a)(3) and (a)(4) of this rule;

(iv) the power, upon request of the chief judge of any circuit or district, or sua sponte, in the event of natural disaster, civil disobedience, or other emergency situation requiring the closure of courts or other circumstances inhibiting the ability of litigants to comply with deadlines imposed by rules of procedure applicable in the courts of this state, to enter such order or orders as may be appropriate to suspend, toll, or otherwise grant relief from time deadlines imposed by otherwise applicable statutes and rules of procedure for such period as may be appropriate, including, without limitation, those affecting speedy trial procedures in criminal and juvenile proceedings, all civil process and proceedings, and all appellate time limitations;

(v) the authority to directly inform all judges on a regular basis by any means, including, but not limited to, email on the state of the judiciary, the state of the budget, issues of importance, priorities and other matters of stateside interest; furthermore, the chief justice shall routinely communicate

with the chief judges and leaders of the district courts, circuit
and county court conferences by the appropriate means;

(vi)   the responsibility to exercise reasonable efforts to promote
and encourage diversity in the administration of justice; and

(vii) the power to perform such other administrative duties as may
be required and which are not otherwise provided for by law
or rule.[8]

Florida's rules also grant the state's chief justice additional duties related
to judicial conferences, temporary assignments of judges, corrective
actions in response to judicial misconduct, chairing the state's Judicial
Management Council, and other administrative tasks.

Given the degree of variation in formally designated judicial leadership
duties across the states, it is difficult to categorize commonalities. That
said, all chief justices are given some general charge to lead the state judicial branch. Court leaders work with a state court administrator and affiliated staff usually and have a role in choosing the former. In most states
that have judicial councils (38 of 43 states), chief justices chair those policymaking bodies, which advise the state legislature on budgetary issues,
new judgeships, performance standards, case management, procedural
issues, and judicial salaries.[9] In addition, most chief justices can approve
administrative plans for the lower courts. A 2021 survey conducted by the
National Center for State Courts and our supplementary research found
that over 80 percent of sampled chief justices ($N = 29$) have the authority
to assign state judges to temporary positions when necessary.[10] Further,
nearly 90 percent of chief justices in the sample population are authorized
to establish special judicial-related committees as needed.[11]

Beyond these common administrative responsibilities are a variety
of idiosyncratic duties given to chief justices. Some court leaders have
extensive appointment powers that include more than temporary judge
positions. For instance, the chief justice in Oregon appoints the chief
judge of the court of appeals, the presiding judges of the circuit courts,
and the presiding judge of the tax court.[12] Appointment powers for chief
justices can extend beyond the staffing of state courts, to quasi-judicial
officers.[13] For example, chief justices in Arizona, Colorado, Indiana,
and Louisiana appoint members to judicial ethics or disciplinary committees.[14] In Alaska, Colorado, and New Jersey, the chief justice has a
role in choosing commissioners for redistricting commissions.[15] Beyond
appointment, committee membership and leadership by the chief justice can extend outside the judicial council. Chief justices in Ohio and

Delaware lead legislative-judicial advisory committees, and the Mississippi chief justice serves on a five-person legislative backup redistricting committee.[16] Some chief justices oversee specialized task forces, as many did to contemplate state court systems' responses to the COVID-19 pandemic beginning in 2020. Finally, chief justices in Illinois have the sole authority to permit or decline access to books in the state's supreme court library (Caruso 2019).

IMPLIED RESPONSIBILITIES

A summary of formal chief justice responsibilities is instructive, but chief justices also assume several implied duties. These duties arise because the chief justice leads a branch of government that operates within a broader state political environment. As the primary spokesperson for the entire state judiciary, the chief justice acts as a functional representative primarily centered on maintaining cordial relations between the courts and other political elements in the state. While the formal roles of chief justices are important, contacts between a chief justice and a state's governor, legislators, budget officials, and bureaucrats are vital for the health of the judiciary (Tobin 1999). Most important are relations with state policymakers. Although court administrators and other judges also maintain regular contact with lawmakers, the chief justice has a pronounced leadership role in interbranch and public relations. Maintaining collegial relations between courts and legislators is beneficial for the judiciary given its dependence on legislatures for most operating funds (Douglas and Hartley 2003), judicial improvements, and general maintenance. When judicial-legislative relations are tainted, the results can be detrimental to the health and well-being of the judiciary (Wilhelm, Vining, Boldt, and Black 2020).

Chief justices themselves often allude to the importance of their informal responsibilities as spokespeople and caretakers for the courts. Former Iowa Chief Justice W. Ward Reynoldson framed these duties as wide-ranging and difficult.

> You know, when I was chief justice I used to say occasionally that being chief justice is like the Olympic javelin team whose captain won the toss and elected to receive. You have these various constituencies . . . the court, you must get along with the court and they must get along together . . . and the bar, it's important that the bar support the court,

. . . the legislature, and the public. Sometimes that gets to be almost insurmountable.[17]

The importance of chief justices to interbranch relations is clear after several decades of efforts to consolidate judicial leadership and create channels of communication with elected leaders. Interbranch relations were the featured topic at numerous conferences and meetings in the 1980s and 1990s, as both judges and legislators became disenchanted with their collective ability to deal with America's War on Drugs, budget shortfalls, and other persistent problems (Christie and Maron 1991, 43). The need for increased communication from chief justices to lawmakers was one of the key lessons learned in that period (Christie and Maron 1991). Contemporary chief justices operate in an environment where their potential influence is well established and where their effort to guide court systems is often expected.

The Emergence of Chief Justices as Reform Leaders

As a direct consequence of the formal and informal administrative authority vested in the position of state chief justice, individuals who serve in that capacity have a significant role in judicial reform efforts. Chief justices are likely the most consequential figures in judicial reform across the states. Court leaders often work in partnership with court administrators and institutions like the National Center for State Courts or the Conference of Chief Justices to analyze or address the needs of the state judiciary. Many chief justices know more about the defects of the courts than anyone else. As court leaders learn about the problems of the judiciary and accept the responsibility to fix them, creating a reform agenda is an understandable next step for chief justices interested in judicial improvements.

While contemporary chief justices often take a pronounced role in judicial reform, chief justices have not always done so. Lack of central-ized leadership in the past meant that advocacy work was piecemeal and that reform success was less predictable than today. Before judge-advocates took a leading role in institutional maintenance, reform in the judicial branch was rarely a priority for policymakers. Those who turned their attention to the judiciary tended to do so when courts were swept up in broader sociopolitical movements. In the Progressive Era, for example, reformers advanced values related to government efficiency, transparency, and unification. While not court-specific, such goals were perceived by many reformers as ideal for the judiciary and other civic institutions (Dosal, McQueen, and Wheeler 2007). When lawmakers tinkered with courts, they most often focused on judicial selection, access to courts, and structural reforms (Hays and Douglas 2006, 986).

State policymakers were not the only ones to blame for the institutional deficiencies of state court systems, as judges themselves were partially at fault. Many judges guarded their independence jealously and resisted the prospect of courts being transformed into highly bureaucratic agencies with uniform rules and procedures or a clear command structure. Efforts to fix the problems of judicial systems tended to be led by attorneys, bar associations, legal scholars, and independent organizations who perceived the court structures they used as inefficient and outdated (C. B. Graham 1993; Hays and Douglas 2006).

An early and highly influential attempt to define a reform agenda for American courts was Roscoe Pound's 1906 address to the American Bar Association. Then Dean of the University of Nebraska College of Law, Pound argued that much of the blame for widespread dissatisfaction with the courts was attributable to deficiencies in the administration of justice (1906, 448–50). He characterized American courts as "archaic" and referred to the courts' procedures as "behind the times," with the results being inefficiency, inflated costs, and a preoccupation with procedure rather than justice. Pound told his audience that courts were too fragmented and that judicial manpower was often wasted. While his ideas were controversial at the time (Stein 2007), he proposed a cohesive agenda for judicial reform that proved to be influential. In his 1906 address and later writings, Pound argued that the machinery of justice could be improved by reducing congestion and delay, promoting court unification, professionalizing the bench and bar, emphasizing continuing education and training, and adapting new technologies (Gazell 2006, 1030–32).

The organization most often associated with leading 20th-century judicial reform efforts was the American Judicature Society (AJS). Established by a coalition of reformist lawyers and laymen in 1913, the AJS suggested modifications that could overcome weaknesses evidenced in Pound's criticisms of American courts. Their drafts for a model state judiciary in 1914 and 1917 embraced court unification and professional, centralized management of the judicial branch (Berkson 1977, 376–77). The reform efforts of the AJS were influential, and their publication of the *Journal of the American Judicature Society* (retitled *Judicature* in mid-1966) facilitated the study and evaluation of judicial administration. The American Bar Association (ABA) also led the reform movement of the era, often working in tandem with the AJS. In fact, Kagan et al. (1978) speculated that the ABA's endorsement of the AJS model for statewide judiciary in 1962 was one reason that state court reforms were widely adopted in the decade that followed.

The reform agenda of the mid-1900s was heavily influenced by national legal organizations, lawyers, and laypersons interested in more effective courts (Winters 1964). Although a number of earlier federal and state judges participated in limited judicial reform efforts (Medina 1952; Reid 1960), chief justices did not emerge as consistent leaders in court reform until the mid-1950s. The gains of court unification included the centralization of administrative authority in chief justices, supreme courts, judicial councils, and court administrators, positioning judicial leaders as pivotal to reform efforts in many states. In the 1960s and 1970s, numerous organizations related to court reform and court management were established to train court administrators and improve court services (Kasparek 2005, 62–81). The establishment of the National Center for State Courts in 1971 provided important infrastructure that allowed state court systems to develop, promote, and evaluate reform initiatives.

Widespread reform of state judicial systems rippled across the American states during the 1970s and was frequently led by chief justices. Part of that reform momentum can be linked to leadership at the federal level. In that decade, Swindler's review of law reform activities led by chief justices referred to Chief Justice Burger's public requests for judicial modernization and reform as "a new type of activism" for court leaders (Swindler 1972, 241). While some chief justices had been reform leaders in the past (Fish 1973; Reid 1960), Burger's eagerness to engage the public, build reform-minded institutions, and fix the state as well as federal courts reached beyond the goals of his predecessors (Reardon 1986, 11–12; Swindler 1972, 857–58). Burger sought court improvements to meet the demands of a dissatisfied public and of judges who were "trying to operate the courts with crackerbarrel corner grocery methods and equipment" in "the supermarket age" (Burger 1970).

The efforts of Burger and various state chief justices put these leaders at the center of historical movements toward court reform. State chief justices who were granted authority by statute or constitutional provisions often used that power to identify and highlight system flaws, typically with the assistance of professional court administrators and/or a judicial council. Though there is substantial variation, many chief justices embraced such responsibilities with gusto. Indiana Chief Justice Randall T. Shepard described the fundamental reason that a chief might devote time and effort to court reform.

Achieving important systemic change usually requires that judicial leaders, sometimes at the top of the pyramid and sometimes in the rank and file, decide to place themselves at risk in the arenas where change can be made. It requires a determination that those of us on the bench and in the bar can do more justice in individual cases if the court system is better organized. (Shepard 2009b, 672)

Many judicial leaders clearly answered the call to lead "systemic change." For example, Texas Chief Justice Joe R. Greenhill praised Alabama Chief Justice Howell T. Heflin for his efforts to modernize his state's courts.

Beyond question Chief Justice Heflin has been a leader in the betterment of administration of justice in the United States. While there are several areas, the two which are of the greatest significance for me were first, his successful efforts in bringing about a reorganization of the court system in his state: a unified court system with proper court administration. The Alabama plan was not only significant for Alabama, it has been an organization which is most helpful as a good example for other states to follow, or at least to study in depth.[18]

Similar commentaries are abundant. California Chief Justice Phil S. Gibson was described by justice and former colleague Stanley Mosk as "a superb administrator, undoubtedly the best in the history of California and perhaps the best in the country" (Mosk 1984, 507). Gibson is generally credited with leading the modernization of California's justice system during his tenure from 1940 to 1964 (Chernick 1982). New Jersey Chief Justice Richard J. Hughes was praised as "an outstanding judicial administrator, who labored and lobbied effectively to improve the efficiency of the courts" (Belknap 1987, 4). Delaware Chief Justice Daniel L. Herrmann was praised as the state's "first true Chief Administrator of Justice" and was credited with "improved court facilities, expanded judicial manpower with increased compensation, long-range planning, computerized information systems, common administrative policies," and other achievements to improve judicial administration.[19] The reform efforts of New York Chief Judge Judith Kaye were widely praised in summaries of her tenure (e.g., Barnett 2017; Estreicher and Chase 2009; Lippman 2009). This list of justices praised for their reform efforts is not remotely comprehensive.

That being said, some chief justices have not embraced an active role in court reform, despite the trend toward centralization. As Shepard

(2009b, 671) noted, "there were some [chiefs] who just wanted to be the leader and others who wanted to lead somewhere." Nonetheless, modern chief justices clearly have the capacity to lead reform efforts. Some strive for national impact, while others are content to safeguard the justice system within a state's borders.

Conclusion

The role of modern state judicial leaders in court administration and reform is central to understanding the present position of chief justices in the states. Over time, administrative duties have gradually been delegated to court leaders, resulting in a contemporary status quo where chief justices are empowered, by design, to oversee and improve entire state court systems. Efforts to accomplish court improvements bring chief justices out of their courts and into more direct relationship with the state political environment. Like their federal counterparts, the state judiciary "has no influence over either the sword or the purse"[20] and thereby relies on the goodwill of lawmakers to overcome many of its problems. The modern state chief justice is empowered to act as advocate for the state judiciary, and that justice's traditional prestige is bolstered by formal law.

The development of infrastructure to assess and address the needs of the state courts has altered the roles of chief justices over time. The contemporary chief justice is highly engaged in administrative leadership, often devoting the bulk of his or her leadership effort to administrative duties. A century ago, court reform movements were mostly led by activist members of the bar, journalists, or legal scholars. Today, court leaders are supported by court administrators and other professional staff who engage in long-term planning, reform implementation, management of personnel and records, data analysis, and other supporting functions (Linhares 2012). The 20th-century reform movement that stressed the role of chief justices in meeting the need for centralization of judicial oversight bore fruit and continues to define expectations about the extrajudicial behavior of modern chief justices. The next chapter examines such behavior. Specifically, we explore advocacy activities of chief justices seeking judicial improvements.

CHAPTER 4

The Chief Justice as Advocate

On January 15, 2020, Indiana Chief Justice Loretta H. Rush delivered her State of the Judiciary address to an audience including Governor Eric J. Holcomb and a joint session of the Indiana General Assembly. Her report discussed the Hoosier State's progress toward maintaining and reforming the justice system. She addressed Indiana's proliferation of problem-solving courts, bail reform, advances in family law, and a need for greater access to counsel among Indiana's citizens. Rush described the modernization efforts of Indiana courts as well as measures to increase civic engagement by the judiciary (Rush 2020).

The following month, New York Chief Judge Janet M. DiFiore used her 2020 State of the Judiciary address to provide a similar message. However, her report also called for a constitutional amendment reorganizing the Empire State's complex and fragmented judicial system. She argued that New York's court system "does not serve the public well" and that "no rational person would ever" build a judiciary like New York's when starting from scratch (DiFiore 2020). DiFiore argued that New York's courts were inefficient, expensive, and a source of substantial frustration for counsel, litigants, criminal defendants, and other participants in the justice system. She was the latest in a series of New York's chief judges to express similar feelings about the state's court system.

Rush and DiFiore discussed some of the same issues in their commentaries, which also shared a similar organizational flow. Both leaders addressed recent achievements and lingering needs for their court systems. Their addresses were not unusual in substance or style. Both had crafted and delivered such messages before, as had their predecessors. The participation of court leaders in this kind of public advocacy has become ordinary, serving as a hallmark of interbranch relations in many states. Such advocacy work is a direct consequence of the administrative and reform leadership expected of modern chief justices.

Public communications by court leaders are part of an ongoing dialogue between the judiciary and other stakeholders in the state political environment. Interaction between the judicial and legislative branches is central to the "cooperative oversight" that links courts to other political institutions (Barrow and Walker 1988). Such communications are vital for the maintenance of a state's justice system. State legislators control the government's policy agenda and its purse strings but are often unfamiliar with the judiciary's problems or how to solve them (Friesen 1977). Consider comments by Delaware chief justice Charles L. Terry, who argued, "Without question, the most immediate cause of [judicial] problems is an utterly shameful legislative neglect, if not outright disinterest" (Terry 1964). A chief justice can articulate judges' needs and broaden awareness of them. Judges and their allies must educate policymakers and the public about judicial functions and must persuade political elites about what is needed to sustain or improve the performance of state courts.

The role of the chief justice is pronounced in an advocacy scenario, given the chief's administrative responsibilities and leadership role. Wisconsin chief justice Shirley S. Abrahamson acknowledged the advocacy aspect of her office when she remarked that being the chief justice "make[s] her the face of the court in the public's eyes" (Shaw 2013). While other judges, court administrators, bar associations, and legal organizations help to develop policies that a chief justice can endorse and promote, the high court's leader is the primary spokesperson for the state justice system (Glick 1970; Tobin 1999). Accordingly, chief justices are the chief advocates for the state judiciary. They frequently use their public communications to highlight both accomplishments and problems, as did Chief Justice Rush and Chief Judge DiFiore in their State of the Judiciary addresses. Public advocacy can generate popular and legislative interest in the judiciary and its top priorities.

Chief justices consider public communications and advocacy efforts to be important aspects of their jobs. For example, Daniel E. Wathen explained that becoming chief justice of Maine was a radical departure from his prior roles as a superior court judge and associate justice.

A Chief Justice is more than a judge—I was now a public figure and the head of a branch of Maine government. The confirmation process functioned as an abbreviated political campaign in that it exposed me to public debate on a number of issues of public policy. I had to walk a narrow line to stay out of the political process, but communications, both internal and external to the court system, were now a major part of my job. (Wathen 2005, 457)

Wathen rated his annual State of the Judiciary address as both his most important communication with the legislature and his favorite task as chief justice (Wathen 2005, 459).

We may not know the degree to which Wathen's sentiments are shared by other chief justices, but court leaders in the modern era frequently act as administrative heads, liaisons, and lobbyists for the state judicial branch. These roles, often public-facing, may be the most important duties of modern court leaders. The advocacy work of the chief justice is highly consequential given its impact on the entire judicial system rather than on just a singular court or case outcome. This consequential impact is a key motivation for the research focus of this book.

In this chapter, we focus on the role of the chief justice as chief advocate for the judicial branch. We examine the public activities of chief justices as they promote judicial reform with efforts aimed at those who have the ability and authority to create responsive policies. We give particular attention to State of the Judiciary addresses delivered by court leaders to an audience typically comprised of state lawmakers, attorneys, or judges. We posit that these messages are key agenda-setting devices for state chief justices. The addresses lay out both the needs of the judiciary for routine upkeep and a chief justice's agenda for reform. They serve as the public presentation of the chief justice's highest judicial priorities and provide chief justices with opportunities to generate interest and support for policies that are consequential for the state judiciary.

The Need for Advocacy and a Public Face

Our previous chapter confirmed that the administrative responsibilities of state chief justices are substantial and multifaceted. Much of their administrative work is done in forums inhabited by individuals who speak the same "judicial" language. However, chief justice activities outside of these venues are also vital aspects of judicial leadership and court administration.

The public activities of modern chief justices on behalf of their court systems are significant for leadership of the state judiciary. Scholars now regularly recognize the agenda-setting and lobbying functions of chief justices (Hartley 2014; Marcin and Marion 2019; Wilhelm, Vining, Boldt, and Trochesset 2019). While codes of conduct limit judges' activities as lobbyists, judges have substantial freedom to advocate for improvements to judicial administration (Hartley 2014; McKoski 2014). That freedom allows judges to endorse policy changes affecting court infrastructure, budgets, personnel, caseloads, and so forth. A chief justice becomes the obvious public advocate for the state judiciary, given the specialized knowledge, formal duties, and prestige of the position. By virtue of the bully pulpit at a chief's disposal, a chief justice has more opportunity for public attention than other potential court advocates.

There are a variety of reasons that chief justices have gained prominence as advocates for state courts. In our last chapter, we discussed how chief justices increasingly became involved in judicial administration and reform as administrative centralization and court unification became commonplace. Modern chief justices are accustomed to having administrative responsibilities and to participating in dialogue with policymakers. Moreover, modern innovations like accountability courts, centralized court budgeting, mandatory sentencing laws, and public defense systems have expanded the universe of issues overseen by chief justices. Judicial leaders clearly have a vested stake in program development and oversight.

The public activities of chief justices suggest that judicial leaders understand and exercise their advocacy roles. Their statements can take the form of public appeals for more funding, judgeships, or infrastructure improvements, but they may also include defending court systems that are the target of rhetorical attacks or court-sanctioning legislation. These events tend to happen when courts face backlash following controversial court rulings or personal failings. In 1998, for example, New Hampshire chief justice David A. Brock went public in his State of the Judiciary address to defend his court after legislative backlash to its controversial 1997 decision in *Claremont School District v. Governor of New Hampshire* (142 N.H. 462, 465, 703 A.2d 1353, 1354). The court ruling against New Hampshire's school finance system angered many policymakers. Brock argued, "When the court is interpreting our Constitution, the statutes passed by our Legislature or court rulings, it is performing the essence of the judicial function interpreting the law" (Berger 1998). His effort to reframe the New Hampshire court's judicial interpretation in an apolitical light is consistent with how many chief justices respond to similar criticism, particularly when speaking to a wider, nonjudicial audience.

Chief justices also promote policies or behaviors that are not derived explicitly from their administrative roles. This activity is consistent with chief justices acting as "justice leaders" (Raftery 2017). For example, during nationwide protests following the death of George P. Floyd Jr., a Black man from Minnesota killed by a police officer, California chief justice Tani G. Cantil-Sakauye issued a statement acknowledging the right to equal justice in America.

> I am deeply disturbed by the tragic deaths of George Floyd and others, as well as the action and inaction that led to these deaths. Justice is the first need addressed by the People in the preamble of our nation's Constitution. As public servants, judicial officers swear an oath to protect and defend the Constitution. We must continue to remove barriers to access and fairness, to address conscious and unconscious bias—and yes, racism. All of us, regardless of gender, race, creed, color, sexual orientation or identity, deserve justice. Our civil and constitutional rights are more than a promise, a pledge, or an oath—we must enforce these rights equally. Being heard is only the first step to action as we continue to strive to build a fairer, more equal and accessible justice system for all. (Allen 2020)

Cantil-Sakauye's statement contributed to a national conversation about race, law enforcement, and the justice system. The chief justices of Hawaii, Indiana, Kentucky, Louisiana, Maryland, New York, and North Carolina issued similar statements.[1]

Reaction to the COVID-19 pandemic provides another example. Ohio chief justice Maureen O'Connor appeared on a July 2020 public television program to discuss the functions of courts during the pandemic. She reviewed the historical racial disparities of the justice system, the need for data collection to analyze equity in Ohio's state courts, the benefits of cameras in courtrooms, bail reform, and the need to "demystify the courts" via public outreach. Attracting statewide media coverage, though, were her comments about mask mandates in Ohio.

> People will tell you, "I have a right not to wear a mask. I have a right not to do this or I have a right to do this" or whatever, and nobody focuses on their duty. What's your duty to society? What's your duty to your community? You know? Your right not to wear a mask and poten-

tially spread disease—what about your duty to your fellow Ohioans? (Kasler 2020)

The preceding examples illustrate the many ways that modern chief justices are more than leaders within the state's highest court. They are also spokespersons, lobbyists, and liaisons for the state court systems. They have public roles that require interaction with the public, policymakers, judges, the bar, journalists, legal organizations, and other parties.

The Chief Advocate and the Modern Judicial Agenda

It is important to understand the agendas chief justices construct as they embrace public advocacy for the judiciary. These agendas are the sets of proposals that court leaders introduce or support to improve the conditions of courts, judges, and participants in the justice system. We are interested in what constitutes these reform agendas and how they vary across the American states.

Ours is not the first research to focus on judicial reform priorities. Rather than observe public activities of chief justices to gauge judicial policy priorities, several scholars have employed surveys of justices (both chiefs and associates) to learn about their goals. Glick (1970) identified nine categories of policy priorities of state supreme courts, with the majority (59.5 percent) revealing substantial interest in judicial reform. Tobin and Hoffman's (1979) survey of 20 state supreme courts, mostly conducted through interviews with state chief justices, discovered widespread concern about judicial administration. In those initial survey analyses, court leaders most frequently focused on trial court unification, personnel administration, improving court facilities, financing court operations, and creating intermediate appellate courts. A second tier of concerns included an insufficient number of trial judges, judicial and continuing legal education, television in courts, and attorney discipline. The remaining needs of courts included reform to the selection of state court administrators, judicial salaries, the use of retired judges, judicial conduct, and uniformity in fines and fees (Tobin and Hoffman 1979, 13).

Surveys conducted in recent decades reveal that some issues have remained judicial priorities (Glick 1982; Dubois and Boyum 1993; Hays and Douglas 2006, 1008–12). Additional moves toward court unification and the centralization of judicial authority are no longer top priorities in many states after the reforms of the past half century, but some states (e.g., New York) still grapple with these issues regularly. Chief justices continue to consider perennial issues like budgeting, state funding, judicial pay, judicial selection, and judicial discipline and removal, but the nature of the judicial agenda has largely turned to reform that is incremental rather than comprehensive (Hays and Douglas 2006, 1012).

Surveys of court leaders provided scholars with the general tenor of judicial priorities while chief justices were taking a more prominent role in administrative leadership. Unquestionably, such surveys of chief justices provide significant insight. Now, decades of overt advocacy activities permit us to analyze what priorities are emphasized by the chief justices when announcing their goals and preferences in public settings. The observable actions of the chief justices provide information about the agenda items that chief justices are willing or eager to advocate rather than just acknowledge. Telling a pollster that an issue is important is different than using leadership capital (political, social, or otherwise) to advocate for that issue.

To examine chief justice advocacy efforts, it is important to analyze activities that are presented in a format that is comparable and relatively generalizable. For a variety of reasons discussed in the next section, we analyzed the content of State of the Judiciary messages. These reports provide insights about the needs of individual state court systems, trends among state courts, and the preferences of judicial branch leaders. As chief justices in the states have transitioned into broader leadership roles, State of the Judiciary messages have captured how they use their authority and status to behave as advocates on behalf of their court systems within the broader state political environment.

The State of the Judiciary Address

State of the Judiciary reports are analogous to other agenda-setting messages in the political world, including State of the Union addresses, governors' State of the State speeches, and the Year-End Report on the Federal Judiciary released annually by the Chief Justice of the United States. State of the Judiciary remarks are delivered in multiple venues, but they are most often speeches by a state chief justice to the state legislature (and sometimes the governor), bar groups, or an assembly of judges. On rare occasions, they are delivered to journalists (e.g., the Tennessee

Press Association in 2011), social clubs (e.g., Oregon chief justices at the Salem City Club), or professional organizations (e.g., the North Carolina Citizens for Business and Industry in 2003). Some are written remarks, and in recent years some have been delivered via online streaming video services such as YouTube (primarily due to the COVID-19 pandemic of 2020 and 2021). Content of State of the Judiciary reports tends to highlight the accomplishments of state courts and to tell the audience about the current challenges of the justice system. The messaging of the reports is intended to help the public and policymakers understand the third branch of government and take an interest in its problems that might otherwise be overlooked or ignored.

State of the Judiciary addresses are the most uniform and visible example of public communications from the state chief justices. While regular messages about the status of the court system are relatively modern phenomena, the notion that there should be regular channels of communication between state courts and policymakers is not of recent vintage. Willoughby (1929, 344) suggested communication between chief justices and other elites long before they became a reality.

> In the same way that the individual courts or judges should make reports to the chief justice in his capacity as administrator in chief of the system, so the latter should prepare and submit to the legislature at least an annual administrative report regarding the operations of the judicial establishment as a whole. This will give to the legislature the information upon which to base its action in providing for the growing needs of the service or in correcting defects in existing organization and procedure which it should be the duty of the chief justice to point out.

By the 1930s, judicial councils in at least 28 states, usually including the chief justice, issued reports on the ongoing business and needs of state courts (see Warner 1937, note 24). Administrative reports providing details about the work of the state courts entered regular use in the 1940s to 1970s. The 1947 revision of the New Jersey Constitution created a new Administrative Office of the Courts to assist the chief justice with oversight and management of the state's judiciary (McConnell 1960; Woelper 1953). Among the many tasks assigned to the state's first administrative director of the courts, Edward B. McConnell, was the annual compilation of "a comprehensive report on the work of all of the courts" of New Jersey (McConnell 1960, 293). The first such compilation was *The Annual*

Report of the Administrative Director of the Courts of New Jersey, 1948–1949.
The administrative director's reports were distributed widely within state
government to aid long-term planning for the court system. McConnell
argued that "reliable statistics on the work of the courts are indispensable
for intelligent administration" and "often more reliable than subjective
impressions obtained by personal observation" (1960, 293).

State chief justices rarely offered personal remarks on the state of the
courts before the 1970s. At a 1920 meeting of the Louisiana Bar Association, Chief Justice Frank A. Monroe participated in a "Symposium on
the Appellate Courts" that focused on "the condition of the judiciary,"
delays in case processing, and the need for a discretionary docket for his
court ("Proceedings of the Twenty-Third Annual Meeting of the Louisiana Bar Association" 1920). The 1962 program of the Virginia Judicial
Conference explicitly featured a "report on the judicial system in Virginia" by Chief Justice John W. Eggleston (Virginia State Bar 1962).[2] The
Washington Post published a brief Associated Press article on the speech,
noting that Eggleston discussed the efficiency of Virginia's courts, growing caseloads in population centers, and the legislature's recent creation
of a new judgeship (Associated Press 1962). The speeches that chief justices gave at subsequent Virginia Judicial Conference meetings resemble
modern State of the Judiciary reports but did not bear that title until the
mid-1970s. Bar journals, law reviews, press coverage, and law libraries of
supreme courts contain little evidence that talks about the condition of
the courts happened often in the late 1960s. When asked, chief justices
of that era reported that their primary pathways to inform legislators and
the public were not direct contacts (Glick 1970).

The need for a mechanism for state judicial leaders to express their
reform requests was apparent to many members of the bench and bar
after Chief Justice Warren E. Burger gave his address titled "The State of
the Judiciary—1970" to the American Bar Association. Early in 1971, the
president of the Indiana Bar Association, John A. Kendall, argued that
Hoosiers should have the opportunity to hear from their courts about
the well-being of the state's judiciary via an annual address. Kendall
believed that such a speech would be appropriate given the broad reach
of the judiciary and limited public knowledge about it. He suggested an
annual report analogous to a State of the Union or State of the State
address, with the chief justice offering remarks about the judiciary to the
legislature (Kendall 1971). Indiana's chief justices began delivering such
remarks in 1973, when Chief Justice Norman F. Arterburn spoke to the
state's legislature.

The motivation to establish a channel of interbranch communication was clear given the historical difficulties of attracting attention to the needs of courts. Ernest C. Friesen, former director of the Institute for Court Management, explained that "the legislature is largely unaware of the day-to-day problems and needs of the courts because it does not generally have the same access to courts as it does to agencies in the other governmental branches. Complementing this is the reluctance of the judiciary to appear to risk its independence by involving itself in the political arena" (Friesen 1977, 41). Despite any such reluctance, many state chief justices followed Burger's lead and began to make public speeches about the condition of state court systems. Numerous early State of the Judiciary reports cite Burger's example.

Formal State of the Judiciary speeches given to state legislators began in 1971, with two states inviting chief justices to give them (Bailey and Uppal 1976). Several other chief justices delivered similar speeches to bar groups or judges in 1971 or soon after. In the opening paragraph of a 1983 address to the New Hampshire legislature, Chief Justice John W. King succinctly described the purpose of his State of the Judiciary speech.

This report serves a very important purpose. It affords the judicial branch of government a special and formal opportunity to thank a co-equal branch of government for their past support, and also acquaints you with our contemporary problems and plans to discharge our constitutional responsibilities to the people of New Hampshire in providing a fair, just and efficient judicial system. (King 1983, 435)

The first chief justice to deliver a State of the Judiciary address to a joint session of a state legislature was Edward E. Pringle of Colorado. On February 8, 1971, a United Press International story acknowledged the occasion as "the first of its kind in any state." Pringle used the speech to defend Colorado's judiciary against public criticism of courts, praise recent court reorganization, celebrate the state's probation system, and warn that some local courts faced substantial backlogs (B. Smith 1971). Pringle was a prominent leader in judicial reform and hoped to establish a formal mechanism to keep legislators aware of the activities and flaws of Colorado's courts.[3]

Soon after Pringle's speech, Michigan chief justice Thomas M. Kavanagh delivered the first State of the Judiciary address before his state's legislature, in March 1971. Reflecting sentiments expressed by Pound and Vanderbilt decades earlier, Kavanagh devoted substantial attention to outdated court practices, case backlogs, insufficient manpower, and funding shortages. In a turn of phrase reminiscent of Chief Justice Burger's quip the year before about modern courts using outdated "crackerbarrel corner grocery methods" (Burger 1970), Kavanagh said that "while astronauts walk the moon, our judicial machinery chugs and lurches along like a Model T"—a fitting remark for the crowd of Michigan legislators (Kavanagh 1971).

In his 1974 State of the Judiciary address, Chief Justice Daniel L. Herrmann told his audience at the Delaware Joint Bench-Bar Conference that such reports were "a fast growing trend" in America. He explained that similar reports had been delivered to a joint session of the legislature in about 12 states and to state bar associations in about 4 states. Herrmann expressed hope that an invitation to deliver an address to the Delaware legislature would be forthcoming.

By the mid-1970s, State of the Judiciary messages were relatively common. In 1976, *The Book of the States* reported that 24 states had initiated a regular State of the Judiciary address (Bailey and Uppal 1976). Two years later, Uppal (1978) found that 32 states' chief justices delivered State of the Judiciary addresses, with the majority given to state legislatures and with most others given to state bar associations. Rausch (1981, 42) reported that State of the Judiciary addresses were delivered in at least 25 states in 1980 or early 1981, with two-thirds of them delivered to an audience of legislators and with the remainder given to the state bar or judicial conference.[4]

The earliest State of the Judiciary or equivalent message we identified in each state is listed in table 4.1. We located those reports using bar journals, law journals, media reports, government publications, and contacts with state high courts and state law libraries. The earliest report we identified that fits the typical content and style of a State of the Judiciary message was published in Colorado. A written report titled *The State of the Courts: Annual Report of the Chief Justice of the Colorado Supreme Court* was released beginning in January 1961 as required by statute. Our investigation reveals that 40 states' court leaders released such a message before 1980—even more than identified by Uppal (1978) or Rausch (1981) in their studies. Court leaders in all 50 states have released similar reports.

Many of these initial messages ($N = 23$) were delivered to state bar meetings.[5] Sixteen of them were oral reports to state legislatures, sometimes with other government officials in attendance.[6] The remaining early State of the Judiciary reports we found were written or oral messages to more idiosyncratic audiences. Chief justices from a trio of states

Table 4.1. Earliest Identified State of the Judiciary Report or Equivalent in Each State

State	Year	Court leader	State	Year	Court leader
AL	1972	Howell T. Heflin	MT	1977	Paul G. Hatfield
AK	1972	George F. Boney	NE	1977	Paul W. White
AZ	1981	Fred C. Struckmeyer Jr.	NV	1975[a]	E. M. "Al" Gunderson
AR	1998	W. H. "Dub" Arnold	NH	1973	Frank R. Kenison
CA	1978[a]	Rose E. Bird	NJ	1977	Richard J. Hughes
CO	1961	Leonard V. B. Sutton	NM	1982[a]	H. Vern Payne
CT	1973	Charles S. House	NY	1974	Charles D. Breitel
DE	1974	Daniel L. Herrmann	NC	1988	James G. Exum Jr.
FL	1971	B. K. Roberts	ND	1973	Ralph J. Erickstad
GA	1971	Bond Almand	OH	1973	C. William O'Neill
HI	1981	William S. Richardson	OK	1972	William A. Berry
ID	1977	Joseph J. McFadden	OR	2007	Paul J. De Muniz
IL	1971	Robert C. Underwood	PA	1971	John C. Bell Jr.
IN	1973	Norman F. Arterburn	RI	2002	Frank J. Williams
IA	1979	W. Ward Reynoldson	SC	1976	J. Woodrow Lewis
KS	1972	Harold R. Fatzer	SD	1977	Francis G. Dunn
KY	1978	John S. Palmore	TN	1971	Ross W. Dyer
LA	1977	Joe W. Sanders	TX	1977	Joe R. Greenhill
ME	1971	Armand A. Dufresne Jr.	UT	1984	Gordon R. Hall
MD	1972	Hall Hammond	VT	1978	Albert W. Barney
MA	1971	G. Joseph Tauro	VA	1975	Lawrence W. I'Anson
MI	1971	Thomas M. Kavanagh	WA	1977	Charles T. Wright
MN	1975	Robert J. Sheran	WV	1973	Thornton G. Berry, Jr.
MS	1978	Neville Patterson	WI	1971	E. Harold Hallows
MO	1971	James A. Finch Jr.	WY	1986	Richard V. Thomas

[a] Klein and Witztum (1973) reported that California, Nevada, and New Mexico court leaders produced State of the Judiciary messages or their equivalent as early as 1972 and (in note 62) that the reports were on file with the Institute of Judicial Administration at New York University School of Law. Institute administrators we contacted indicated that they no longer maintain such records, and we were unable to identify or locate such reports or additional references to confirm their format or existence.

(Texas, Virginia, and Wisconsin) gave State of the Judiciary speeches to state judicial conferences. Two states' first reports were given at Bench-Bar conferences with attorneys and judges in attendance (Delaware and Mississippi). The chief justice of Illinois provided a written report as early as 1971. The most unusual settings for early State of the Judiciary reports were the Arkansas Trial Practice Institute, the National College of the State Judiciary (Nevada in 1975), the New Mexico Judicial Council, and the Salem City Club (Oregon in 2007). Venues for the messages have changed frequently over time, as discussed below.

SOJ: OPPORTUNITY

Chief justices recognize that reports to policymakers and other audiences provide opportunities to promote their agendas and the well-being of state courts. The potential utility of State of the Judiciary addresses for interbranch communication was touted decades ago by Delaware chief justice Andrew D. Christie and judicial-legislative relations consultant Nancy C. Maron. While reporting the recommendations from a 1989 conference on interbranch relations, they emphasized the need to "expand the scope and use of formal communication mechanisms, such as state of the judiciary addresses and joint meetings" with policymakers (Christie and Maron 1991, 16). They deemed it vital for the judiciary to speak "with a unified voice" when advancing a platform for institutional change and maintenance. Christie and Maron reported that State of the Judiciary addresses were becoming more common at the time, with chief justices often using them to "urge interbranch cooperation to solve issues of mutual concern" (17).

Many other court leaders aside from Christie have expressed their awareness that a State of the Judiciary address is an important opportunity for advocacy. In 1986, California chief justice Rose E. Bird delivered her report to the state bar convention while facing death threats, illness, and an election that would ultimately remove her from office. Although she had to enter through a side door accompanied by state police and leave promptly after completing her remarks, Bird fulfilled her commitment to inform the audience about the challenges faced by the bench and bar (Milstein 1986). Chief Justice Leigh I. Saufley reflected on the importance of such events in her 2017 address to the Maine legislature: "We don't take this tradition for granted. It doesn't happen in every state, and the benefits of formal communication between the separate, but equal branches of government can't be overstated. So very much has been accomplished in the last decade because of the work that we have all done together" (Saufley 2017).

Some chief justices have used guests or unique formats to draw attention to their State of the Judiciary reports. Missouri chief justice Edward D. Robertson generated excitement about his 1992 address by inviting a special visitor to participate. At Robertson's request, All-Pro Kansas City Chiefs linebacker Derrick Thomas told the Missouri legislators how Florida's juvenile laws had guided him away from unlawful behavior and toward a successful adulthood. Thomas recommended that Missouri adopt laws similar to those that helped him in the Sunshine State (Sentell

1992). Chief Judge Judith S. Kaye of New York delivered her 1997 State of the Judiciary message in the form of a tabloid newspaper that included a crossword puzzle. Kaye, a former journalist, explained that the format was intended to engage her audience in a more interesting way than her usual "real snooze" of a speech (Caher 1997). In 2013, Chief Justice Mark E. Recktenwald of Hawaii became the first to deliver his State of the Judiciary address via YouTube, doing so on the Hawaii Courts channel.[7] While recordings of other State of the Judiciary speeches had been posted online in earlier years, Recktenwald was the first to speak directly to his online audience rather than sharing video of a traditional speech. During the COVID-19 pandemic of 2020 and 2021, several chief justices shifted their State of the Judiciary speeches online (e.g., in Kansas, Minnesota, Missouri, New York, North Carolina, Utah, and Wyoming). Time will tell whether chief justices embrace online delivery of reports on the judiciary outside of extraordinary circumstances.[8]

SOJ: FREQUENCY AND VENUE

Since state chief justices began providing State of the Judiciary reports, there has been considerable variation in how often these reports are delivered and what audience receives them. The reports are an annual event in some states, a rarity in others. Many chief justices give remarks to a joint assembly of the state legislature and perhaps the governor. Many others give their speeches to meetings of the bar or a collection of judges. Below, we discuss the basis for the practices associated with these reports in the various states.

Frequency. The frequency of State of the Judiciary messages varies across states and over time. In some states, the messages are regular, taking place as routine interactions between chief justices and their audiences. In those states, the reports may be presented annually or every two years and are expected and normal occasions. In other states, State of the Judiciary addresses are irregular or rare.

In many states where State of the Judiciary addresses are regular events, the frequency of the chief justice's report is set by statute. For example, the Texas Government Code mandates,

(a) At a convenient time at the commencement of each regular session of the legislature, the chief justice of the supreme court shall deliver a written or oral state of the judiciary message evaluating the accessibility of the courts to the citizens of the state and the future directions and needs of the courts of the state.

(b) It is the intent of the legislature that the state of the judiciary message promote better understanding between the legislative and judicial branches of government and promote more efficient administration of justice in Texas.[9]

The effect of this statute has been a State of the Judiciary report to the Texas legislature every other year since 1979.

In states without a legal requirement that such a report be provided, it tends to occur at the invitation of the state legislature. The invitation to report may be initiated by either the lawmakers or the chief justice, but the former scenario is more typical. For example, the Maine legislature invited Chief Justice Leigh I. Saufley to the state capitol in 2018 by letter.

Dear Chief Justice Saufley:

We are pleased to invite you to address a Joint Session of the 128th Maine Legislature on Tuesday, February 27, 2018, at 11:00 a.m. concerning the State of the Judiciary and any other matters that you may care to bring to our attention. We look forward to seeing you then.

Sincerely,

S/Michael D. Thibodeau
President *of the* Senate
S/Sara Gideon
Speaker of the House[10]

The reverse scenario, with a chief justice requesting an audience of legislators, took place when Nevada Chief Justice Michael L. Douglas sent a letter in 2011 requesting permission to address his state's legislature.

DEAR SPEAKER OCEGUERA:

Pursuant to past protocol, I would like to request permission, as Chief Justice of the Nevada Supreme Court in 2011, to address a joint session of the Legislature on the State of the Judiciary

on March 7, 2011, at 5:30 p.m. Also, immediately following, the
Court will be hosting its annual reception for the legislators in
the court's rotunda. Your consideration of this request is greatly
appreciated.

Sincerely,

MICHAEL L. DOUGLAS
Chief Justice[11]

Where State of the Judiciary remarks are irregular, it is sometimes
due to the preference of the chief justice. One example occurs in Rhode
Island, a state with no consistent history of State of the Judiciary messages. Rhode Island's Administrative Office of State Courts had issued
a written report on the judiciary annually since 1972 when Chief Justice
Frank J. Williams took the reins of the Rhode Island Supreme Court
in 2001. Consistent with his goals of increasing public awareness and
understanding of his court, Williams delivered an annual State of the
Judiciary speech to the Rhode Island legislature from 2002 to 2008. His
successors have not continued the practice (Moore 2015).

Venue. The venue for State of the Judiciary remarks depends on the preferences of the chief justice as well as the legislative leadership. In Florida,
State of the Judiciary addresses to the state bar have been common. In
1993, Chief Justice Rosemary Barkett requested to deliver a State of the
Judiciary address to the legislature, which no chief justice had done in 16
years. Barkett told Florida legislators that the courts were in dire condition, woefully underfunded, and overworked. Her remarks included an
appeal all too familiar to state chief justices: "I don't come to you today
presuming to ask for a dime—I know that's too much—but simply say to
you: 'Brothers and sisters, could you spare a penny?'" (Bergstrom 1993).
It is apparent that Barkett believed she could emphasize the needs of the
courts more effectively in the state capitol.

While chief justices may prefer a direct audience with state legislators, the feeling is not always mutual. In several notable instances, chief
justices have been uninvited or disallowed from giving State of the Judiciary talks to lawmakers during periods of poor interbranch relations.
These episodes tend to draw attention from journalists and other political observers, sometimes attracting national press coverage. One early
example happened in California during the early 1990s. Despite being

the first California chief justice to give State of the Judiciary remarks in the legislative chamber during 1990 and 1991 (Hager 1990, 1991), Chief Justice Malcom M. Lucas was not permitted to give his address to the legislature in 1992. Legislators were angry after the 1991 decision in *Legislature v. Eu* (54 Cal. 3d 492) upheld Proposition 140, approved by California voters in 1990. That initiative installed term limits for state legislators, eliminated their pension benefits, and slashed the operating budgets of legislators by at least 38 percent (Egelko 2006, 2016; Jacobs 1990). Furious legislators responded to the court's decision by proposing an identical budget cut of 38 percent for the courts, cuts to judicial pensions, and a constitutional amendment to prevent courts from ordering government agencies to pay fines or fund programs. Lucas delivered a State of the Judiciary address to the State Bar of California rather than to the state legislature (Hager 1992).

Additional incidents of this type have occurred more recently. In 2003, North Carolina legislators declined to invite Chief Justice I. Beverly Lake Jr. to continue the practice of giving State of the Judiciary remarks in their House chamber. Republican legislators speculated that the snub was due to lingering unhappiness among Democrats with his court's 2002 ruling in *Stephenson v. Bartlett* (562 S.E.2d 377) that rejected Democrats' state legislative redistricting plans. The state's House and Senate districts supported by the court's ruling were more amenable to electing Republicans (Betts 2003).

Kansas chief justice Lawton R. Nuss was denied the opportunity to address legislators directly from 2013 to 2016, instead delivering his remarks in a written format (in 2013) or at the Kansas Judicial Center (2014 to 2016). Poor judicial-legislative relations were the likely cause of this scenario. Kansas Supreme Court rulings related to education funding, abortion rights, and capital punishment were criticized heavily by legislators. Kansas Speaker of the House and Republican Raymond F. Merrick explained the refusal to host Nuss in 2013 by arguing that the legislature could spend its time on more productive activities: "It's just another thing to take up time. I just think it's time that could be put to better use on other things" (Holman 2013). In February 2016, the House debated a constitutional amendment to change the state's method of judicial selection on the same day Chief Justice Nuss delivered his address (Holman 2016). The tradition was revived in 2017 by Speaker Merrick's successor, Republican Ron Ryckman Jr.

Washington legislators declined to invite Chief Justice Barbara A. Madsen to address them in 2015, breaking a tradition maintained in that state since 1994. The state supreme court had held the state legislature in contempt during 2014 for its failure to fund education adequately. Lawmakers argued that their decision was not driven by political motives, with Republican senator Don Benton arguing that the speech was "a horrible waste of time" and "boring." Madsen expressed her disappointment in a statement to the press, saying she "hope[d] that, in the future, the Supreme Court will again be invited to make this important presentation" (Dake 2015).

Some chief justices voluntarily decline to deliver a State of the Judiciary address to the legislature. For example, Chief Justice Thomas E. McHugh of West Virginia canceled his 1996 address to legislators despite positive responses to prior speeches. McHugh based his choice on a perceived a lack of legislative interest. The chief justice explained that he would deliver his talk to the state bar and West Virginia's judicial association as usual and pursue the court's needs through direct contacts with legislative committees. McHugh's decision was unusual but rooted in the expectation that his advocacy would be just as effective if he gave his speech one less time while also seeking help from lawmakers in different venues (Charnock 1996).

SOJ: CONTENT

The February 1972 edition of *The Third Branch*, the newsletter of the federal courts, reported that some states' chief justices had given State of the Judiciary speeches to legislators that year. It noted four relevant states (Alaska, Maryland, Michigan, and Oklahoma) and the key legislative initiatives requested by their court leaders. From the time the ritual of the address began, its intention was clear—to discuss the accomplishments and status of the courts and to explain what they need to improve their operations. While these messages are not the only venue to do so and chief justices do not act alone to achieve their goals, the messages draw attention to the reform agenda of the courts. They tell policymakers, journalists, and the public what the leader of the court system perceives as necessary to maintain and improve the state judicial system. Although these addresses were largely ignored by scholars for decades (cf. Rausch 1981), they have recently been recognized by practitioners and scholars as important agenda-setting devices (Flango et al. 2015, 6–7; Marcin and Marion 2019; Wilhelm, Vining, Boldt, and Black 2020; Wilhelm, Vining, Boldt, and Trochesset 2019).

The content of the State of the Judiciary reports reflects the reform priorities of chief justices and, by extension, the state judiciaries. For example, Chief Justice Wathen of Maine explained that he was conscientious when developing his aforementioned list of requests to improve the justice system: "Ask and ye shall receive, particularly if you know what to ask for and how to pave the way beforehand. Having established my long-term plans early on, in the last several years I learned to focus on three specific requests annually. I was usually successful and that reinforced the sense that, together we were indeed making progress" (Wathen 2005, 460).

Our analysis of the content of State of the Judiciary reports examined 871 oral or written reports issued by chief justices from 1961 to 2021. A list of all State of the Judiciary reports or equivalent communication included in our data set is provided in table 4.2. We identify whether the report was issued in writing or delivered as a speech to the bar, bench, legislature, or another audience. Forty-nine states are included in our analysis, with an average of 17.42 reports per state (range = 3–47). In our examination of the reports, we categorize a chief justice's comment as a request when it calls for policymakers to take positive or negative action that would enact or reject an initiative relevant to the justice system. We included proposals that are directed at state lawmakers who can enact reforms via the policymaking process rather than at judges or bar groups. In addition, requests were only included in our analysis if the court leader's call to action was sufficiently specific that it gave clear direction to policymakers.

We analyzed the frequency of requests from the policy categories identified in table 4.3. The bulk of these policy types were developed in earlier research on annual reports on the federal judiciary issued by the Chief Justice of the United States (Vining and Wilhelm 2012). They include access to counsel, budget alterations, general legislation, housekeeping, judgeships or staff, salaries and benefits, statutory revisions, structural change, and study requests. We include additional categories for issues that are more specific to the context of state, rather than federal, justice systems. These categories include judicial selection, juvenile justice, and specialty courts.

The frequency of each category of requests is shown in table 4.4. Among the 1,746 total requests in our data, the largest subset addresses general housekeeping for state courts. Such proposals comprise over a quarter of all requests. Many of the housekeeping proposals relate to the repair and maintenance of court facilities, security or technology

Table 4.2. State of the Judiciary Reports in Our Data Set

State	Years (audience)	State	Years (audience)
AL	1972 (bar), 1981 (bench-bar luncheon), 2008–11 (legislature)	MT	1977, 1979, 1981, 1985, 1987, 1989, 1991, 1993, 1995–96, 1998, 2001, 2003, 2005, 2007, 2009, 2011, 2013, 2015 (legislature), 2017 (written), 2019 (legislature)
AK	1978, 1980, 2001–21 (legislature)	NE	1981, 1983, 1985, 2008–21 (legislature)
AZ	1982 (bar), 1986–87, 1989–91, 2001–2, 2005, 2007–11 (legislature)	NV	1976 (National College of the State Judiciary), 1999, 2001, 2003, 2005, 2007, 2009, 2011, 2013, 2015, 2017, 2019 (legislature)
AR	1998 (Arkansas Trial Practice Institute), 2010–14, 2016–20 (bar and judicial council)	NH	1973, 1983 (legislature), 1985–86 (bar), 1987, 1996, 2005, 2007, 2009 (legislature)
CA	1978–89 (bar), 1990 (bar and legislature), 1991 (bar), 1992–95 (bar), 1996 (legislature), 1997–98 (bar and legislature, separately), 1999–2010 (legislature), 2011 (bar), 2012–20 (legislature)	NJ	1977 (legislature), 2002–19 (bar)
CO	1961, 1968–70 (written), 1971 (legislature), 1972 (written), 1973 (legislature), 1974 (bar), 1975, 1977, 1979, 1981, 1983–85, 1987, 1989, 1991, 1993, 1995, 1997, 1999, 2001, 2003, 2005, 2007, 2009, 2011, 2013, 2015, 2017, 2019, 2021 (legislature)	NM	1994, 1996 (legislature), 1997 (bar), 1998, 2005, 2009, 2011, 2013, 2015, 2017, 2019 (legislature)
CT	1999, 2009, 2011, 2017 (legislature)	NY	1988 (written), 1998–2008 (bench and state leaders), 2010 (written), 2011–15, 2017–20 (bench and state leaders), 2021 (virtual)
DE	1974–75, 1990 (bench-bar conference), 1993–94, 1997–98, 2000–2001, 2003–4 (legislature), 2010–13 (written), 2014 (bench-bar conference)	NC	1989 (bar), 1991, 1993, 1995, 1997 (legislature), 1999 (bar), 2001 (legislature), 2003 (bar and professional organization, separately), 2015 (legislature), 2017–20 (bar)
FL	1971–73, 2020 (bar)	ND	1979 (bar), 1991 (legislature), 1993 (bar), 1999, 2001, 2003, 2005, 2007, 2009 (legislature), 2010 (bar), 2011, 2013, 2015, 2017, 2019, 2021 (legislature)

Table 4.2—*Continued*

State	Years (audience)	State	Years (audience)
GA	1971–72 (bar), 2003, 2005–21 (legislature)	OH	1973 (bar), 1987–96 (judicial conference), 1997 (legislature), 1998–2000 (judicial conference), 2001 (legislature), 2002–6 (judicial conference), 2007 (legislature), 2008–20 (judicial conference)
HI	1997–2001, 2003, 2005, 2007 (legislature), 2009 (American Judicature Society), 2010–11 (legislature), 2013 (virtual), 2015, 2017, 2019, 2021 (legislature)	OK	1972 (legislature), 1979 (bar), 1982, 1985, 1987, 1995 (legislature)
ID	1977 (bar), 2005–11 (written), 2013–14, 2016–18, 2020–21 (legislature)	OR	2007–11, 2013–14 (civic organization)
IL	1971 (written), 1982 (judicial conference), 2012 (written)	PA	1971, 1973, 1984 (bar), 1987 (legislature), 2006–14 (written)
IN	1973, 1975–2020 (legislature)	RI	2002–8 (legislature)
IA	1995–2021 (legislature)	SC	1977 (bar), 1985–2019 (legislature)
KS	1972 (legislature), 1973 (bar), 2000–2008 (written), 2009 (legislature), 2010 (written), 2011–12 (legislature), 2013 (written), 2014–16 (state leaders), 2017–19 (legislature), 2020 (virtual)	SD	1977–80 (legislature), 1991–2002 (written), 2003–21 (legislature)
KY	1978, 1980 (legislature), 2010–19 (interim joint committee on the judiciary)	TN	1974, 1980 (bar), 2010 (written), 2011 (journalists)
LA	1977, 1979, 1999, 2001, 2003, 2005, 2007–9, 2011, 2013, 2016, 2018 (legislature)	TX	1979, 1981, 1983, 1985, 1987, 1989, 1991, 1993, 1995, 1997, 1999, 2001, 2003, 2005, 2007, 2009, 2011, 2013, 2015, 2017, 2019 (legislature), 2021 (virtual)
ME	1993–2020 (legislature)	UT	1984, 1990 (bar), 1998–2017, 2019, 2021 (legislature)
MD	1993, 1996–97, 1999–2003, 2005, 2015, 2019 (legislature)	VT	none
MA	1971, 2002–9, 2011–13 (bar), 2014–19 (bench-bar symposium), 2021 (virtual)	VA	1978–86, 1988, 1990–93, 1995–96, 2000–2011 (judicial conference)

Table 4.2—*Continued*

State	Years (audience)	State	Years (audience)
MI	1971, 1984, 1986–88, 1990, 1994–95, 1997, 2000, 2010 (legislature)	WA	1979–80, 1989 (bar), 2000 (written), 2001, 2003, 2005 (legislature), 2006 (written), 2007 (legislature), 2008 (written), 2009 (legislature), 2010 (written), 2011 (legislature), 2012 (written), 2013 (legislature), 2014, 2015 (written), 2019 (legislature)
MN	1978–79, 1981, 1983, 1985–90, 1995, 1998–99, 2001, 2005–10, 2018–20 (bar)	WV	1990 (legislature), 1995, 2001 (bar)
MS	1981 (bar), 1992, 1995 (legislature)	WI	1975, 2000–2003, 2005–20 (judicial conference)
MO	1971 (bar), 1996, 1998–2020 (legislature), 2021 (virtual)	WY	1997, 1999–2021 (legislature)

upgrades, court fees, juror compensation, and use of interpreters. These concerns represent basic needs of courts and judges that wish to maintain effective and efficient facilities and staff in the judicial branch. The second most common category, comprising nearly one in five requests in our data, proposes additional judgeships or staff. Most of these requests were for more judges to assist overburdened courts, but court leaders also asked for more court administrators, probation officers, bailiffs, law clerks, or other support staff. Another common type of request relates to salaries and benefits. Most of these requests were for salary increases, a regular cause for concern among state and federal judges. A smaller proportion of this request type asked for improvements to judicial retirement systems, insurance, or disability benefits.

All other categories of requests are respectively present in less than 10 percent of our data. Proposals for structural change to the state judiciary, primarily focused on court creation or reforming jurisdictions, comprise 8.71 percent of the requests we found. Just over 8 percent of requests were appeals concerned with budgeting. Court leaders frequently asked either for budget increases or for funding at levels consistent with the prior year. Chief justices often acknowledged other demands for state funds but made the case that the courts and associated programs needed adequate funding to serve citizens. Each of four categories of requests—access to counsel, judicial selection, statutory revisions, and specialty

Table 4.3. Types of Requests in State of the Judiciary Reports

Access to counsel	Requests to improve the state's public defense or legal aid system, usually requesting additional funds or personnel
Budget	Requests for specific budget alterations, typically seeking more funds to pay for court operations and personnel
General legislation	Recommendations regarding the legislative approval or disapproval of policy initiatives with an impact on courts but not limited to the judiciary
Housekeeping	Proposals encouraging basic maintenance of the judicial branch, judicial procedure, fee structures, and court-house infrastructure
Judgeships or staff	Requests for more judges or administrative staff, typi-cally due to case backlogs
Judicial selection	Proposals related to the reform of a state's method of selecting, retaining, or removing judges
Juvenile justice	Requests to improve or reform states' systems for the treatment, rehabilitation, or detention of juvenile offenders
Salaries and benefits	Requests related to judicial compensation, typically ask-ing for increases in salaries or benefits
Specialty courts	Recommendations regarding problem-solving courts, including community courts, drug courts, DUI courts, family violence courts, homeless courts, mental health courts, veterans courts, and similar innovations serving as alternatives to criminal courts
Statutory revision	Requests to revise statutory law to alter the impact or functions of some aspect of the justice system
Structural change	Requests to reorganize the judicial system of a state in some way, often including the creation, elimination, or reorganization of courts or their jurisdictions
Study requests	Request to study some aspect of the justice system to assess its efficacy or evaluate the impact of a given reform

courts—comprise approximately 5 percent of the pool we examined. The least common categories of requests were general legislation (2.46 percent), juvenile justice (2.23 percent), and study requests (2.18 percent).

The distribution of the requests we identified suggests that chief justices focus frequently on the immediate needs of courts and judges. Court leaders ask policymakers for assistance with the basic tools needed to keep the judicial machinery in motion and to assure that

Table 4.4. Chief Justice Requests in State of the Judiciary Reports, 1961–2021

Issue area	Total	(percentage)
Access to counsel	95	(5.44%)
Budget	140	(8.02%)
General legislation	43	(2.46%)
Housekeeping ´	439	(25.14%)
Judgeships or staff	317	(18.16%)
Judicial selection	87	(4.98%)
Juvenile justice	39	(2.23%)
Salaries and benefits	226	(12.94%)
Specialty courts	83	(4.75%)
Statutory revision	87	(4.98%)
Structural change	152	(8.71%)
Study requests	38	(2.18%)

Note: N = 1,746.

judicial personnel are adequately compensated. Their requests inform the audience of these needs and of the potential consequences if needs are neglected or ignored (e.g., delays in case processing, turnover among judges and staff, and low institutional morale). Chief justices and chief judges also shine a light on issues with long-term consequences for courts and citizens. Changes to judicial institutions, jurisdictional boundaries, judicial selection systems, and state laws tend to have lasting effects. These reforms are often difficult to achieve and tend to persist once they are enacted.

To better understand how the priorities of chief justices have changed over time, we investigated their primary concerns during each decade from the 1970s to the 2010s. We show the results of our investigation in table 4.5. Several evident patterns indicate gradual change in the agendas of chief justices.

When State of the Judiciary reports were normalized in the 1970s, their content focused most often on judgeships or staff (29.73 percent) and structural change (26.49 percent). Attention to those issues declined gradually during the decades that followed. Requests for more judgeships or staff declined by nearly two-thirds by the 2010s and took a similar tone throughout our data set. Those propositions waned as courts added personnel and developed strategies to increase their efficiency or reduce their workloads (e.g., discretionary dockets, clerks, unpublished opinions, and improved technology). Even more dramatic was the drop

Table 4.5. Chief Justice Requests in State of the Judiciary Reports by Decade, 1970s–2010s

	1970–79	1980–89	1990–99	2000–2009	2010–19
Access to counsel	1	3	6	50	32
	(0.54%)	(2.00%)	(2.26%)	(7.63%)	(7.51%)
Budget	7	4	23	59	43
	(3.78%)	(2.67%)	(8.65%)	(9.01%)	(10.09%)
General legislation	8	4	4	16	9
	(4.43%)	(2.67%)	(1.50%)	(2.44%)	(2.11%)
Housekeeping	26	27	65	188	119
	(14.05%)	(18.00%)	(24.44%)	(28.70%)	(27.93%)
Judgeships or staff	55	31	52	123	43
	(29.73%)	(20.67%)	(19.55%)	(18.78%)	(10.09%)
Judicial selection	4	18	16	31	18
	(2.16%)	(12.00%)	(6.02%)	(4.73%)	(4.23%)
Juvenile justice	2	3	6	14	11
	(1.08%)	(2.00%)	(2.26%)	(2.14%)	(2.58%)
Salaries and benefits	19	23	31	78	64
	(10.27%)	(15.33%)	(11.65%)	(11.91%)	(15.02%)
Specialty courts	1	0	15	27	38
	(0.54%)	(0.00%)	(5.64%)	(4.12%)	(8.92%)
Statutory revision	10	3	12	26	33
	(5.41%)	(2.00%)	(4.51%)	(3.97%)	(7.75%)
Structural change	49	28	30	26	11
	(26.49%)	(18.67%)	(11.28%)	(3.97%)	(2.58%)
Study requests	3	6	6	17	5
	(1.62%)	(4.00%)	(2.26%)	(2.60%)	(1.17%)
	$N = 185$	$N = 150$	$N = 266$	$N = 655$	$N = 426$

in proposals for structural change. Early requests for structural change tended to focus on the creation of intermediate appellate courts, the establishment of court administrators and associated personnel, and court unification. Many of those issues were resolved by the 1980s or 1990s, when prevalence rose for reforms related to jurisdiction, court consolidation, and sources of court funding. By the 2000s and 2010s, the heightened attention to reorganizing or creating courts had dissipated substantially.

Several categories of requests became more common over time in response to contemporaneous conditions. These categories include proposals related to housekeeping, access to counsel, budget, and specialty courts. Housekeeping requests became the most common type of request by the 1990s, as the courts emerged from sweeping changes of the prior decades. Access to counsel received little attention in messages from chief justices before the 2000s but later rose in prominence. The bulk of those requests focus on inadequacies in the existing system for indigent defense, with the emphasis on either greater funding or a broader pool of eligible attorneys. The rate of requests for budget stability or increases more than doubled by the 1990s and continued to increase in the following decades. Specialty courts were mostly absent from the agendas of chief justices before the 1990s. The initial burst of interest in those programs focused on both family courts and drug courts, with the latter getting more attention by the 2000s. That shift is consistent with the general trajectory of drug courts, which have become very common throughout the United States in response to overcrowded correctional facilities and an emphasis on rehabilitation. Accountability courts became a relatively frequent subject of attention from court leaders, with nearly 1 in 11 of their requests in the 2010s focused on drug courts, mental health courts, and similar programs.

The category of requests with the most irregular trajectory concerned judicial selection systems. Such requests were rare in the 1970s (2.16 percent of the total) but increased to 12 percent of proposals from court leaders in the 1980s. Comprising nearly all of that 12 percent were pleas to adopt merit selection of judges or to otherwise abandon partisan judicial elections. Beginning in the 1990s, proposals related to picking and retaining judges steadily occupied between 4.23 percent and 6.02 percent of requests by chief justices and chief judges. The topics of those appeals were more diverse, though court leaders continued to advocate for merit selection. They also addressed redistricting and campaign finance reform for judicial elections and modifying term lengths for judges.

Other issues were present at a relatively consistent rate throughout the five decades in our data. Among these topics, the most prominent was salaries and benefits for judicial branch employees, particularly judges. Requests on that topic comprised 10.27 percent to 15.33 percent of the agenda during each decade. Proposals for statutory revisions fluctuated between 2 percent and 7.75 percent of the total agenda in each decade. These commented on a variety of topics, with particular attention to sentencing reform, bail reform, reclassifying criminal offenses, and procedural reform. Requests to adopt or reject pending legislation were less common. They occupied 4.43 percent of the agenda in the 1970s but only 1.50 percent to 2.67 percent of the data set from later decades. Numerous topics were present in these requests, with most related to services for vulnerable populations (e.g., children, the mentally ill, and the disabled), allocation of funds to nonjudicial entities, or the adoption or elimination of criminal or civil offenses. Study requests were among the least frequent types of proposals throughout the entire time period we examined. At no point did they exceed 4 percent of the total requests, and they were typically even less common. These proposals tended to recommend studies or pilot programs related to issues such as court workloads, long-term planning for the judiciary, and court services for certain populations (e.g., children, the elderly, and families). Another relatively rare subject in pleas from chief justices was juvenile justice. Their requests in that arena drew attention to a variety of flaws in the juvenile justice system. Common topics included funding and staff increases for that system, pay for attorneys representing juveniles, and revisions to the juvenile code.

Table 4.6. Chief Justice Requests in State of the Judiciary Reports by State, 1961–2021

State	Average requests per report	Most common request (percentage of total)	State	Average requests per report	Most common request (percentage of total)
AL	4.33	Statutory revisions (46.15%)	MT	0.95	Judgeships and staff (30.00%)
AK	1.26	Housekeeping (27.59%)	NE	0.88	Housekeeping (26.67%)
AZ	1.57	Housekeeping (45.45%)	NV	1.75	Housekeeping / judgeships and staff (23.81%)
AR	0.81	Housekeeping / salaries and benefits (33.33%)	NH	2.11	Housekeeping (42.11%)
CA	1.72	Housekeeping (32.43%)	NJ	0.95	Housekeeping (33.33%)
CO	4.45	Judgeships and staff (38.78%)	NM	2.36	Budget (30.77%)
CT	0.25	Housekeeping (100%)	NY	4.09	Housekeeping (23.40%)
DE	4.63	Structural change (21.62%)	NC	0.77	Housekeeping (60%)
FL	1.50	Statutory revisions / structural change (33.33%)	ND	2.00	Housekeeping (34.38%)

Table 4.6—*Continued*

State	Average requests per report	Most common request (percentage of total)	State	Average requests per report	Most common request (percentage of total)
GA	1.75	Statutory revisions (22.86%)	OH	0.83	Salaries and benefits (27.59%)
HI	3.50	Housekeeping (33.93%)	OK	2.17	Salaries and benefits (30.77%)
ID	1.67	Housekeeping (36.00%)	OR	2.71	Housekeeping (36.84%)
IL	0.33	Salaries and benefits (100%)	PA	0.46	Judicial selection (33.33%)
IN	1.49	Housekeeping / structural change (24.29%)	RI	2.00	Housekeeping (50.00%)
IA	2.07	Housekeeping (25.00%)	SC	1.47	Housekeeping (30.19%)
KS	3.52	Judgeships and staff (44.44%)	SD	0.97	Budget (23.53%)
KY	2.58	Salaries and benefits (35.48%)	TN	0.25	Housekeeping (100%)
LA	2.31	Judgeships and staff (26.67%)	TX	3.95	Judicial selection (24.14%)
ME	2.71	Housekeeping (42.67%)	UT	1.21	Judgeships and staff (20.69%)
MD	6.81	Judgeships and staff (41.33%)	VT	none	none
MA	1.47	Housekeeping (28.57%)	VA	1.46	Judicial selection (21.95%)
MI	2.00	Judgeships and staff (30.43%)	WA	3.64	Housekeeping (37.25%)
MN	1.13	Structural change (23.08%)	WV	1.00	Salaries and benefits (66.67%)
MS	0.00	none	WI	0.86	Salaries and benefits (33.33%)
MO	1.85	Housekeeping (39.58%)	WY	1.88	Housekeeping (46.67%)

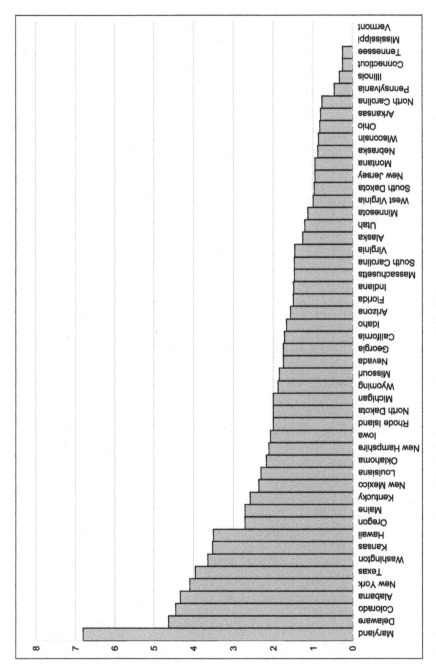

Fig. 6. Average requests per State of the Judiciary report by state, 1961–2021

There was also substantial variation among the states. In table 4.6, we show the average number of requests per report in each state and the most common issue invoked by each state's chief justice or chief judge. In figure 6, we display the number of requests per state from most to least. The mean of two requests per report indicates that chief justices in the various states tend to focus on a narrow set of key needs rather than presenting an extensive wish list. However, we identified substantial differences in the number of requests in each state. Twenty states exceeded the mean of two requests per speech, with chief justices in the remainder of states limiting their requests to fewer priorities. The chief judges of Maryland had the most proposals per report, asking for nearly seven initiatives per message. Many of those proposals were specific requests for additional judgeships or staff. Chief justices or chief judges in four states asked for at least four requests per speech, and Texas chief justices nearly reached that standard (with 3.95 requests per report). The leaders of these court systems included several chief justices with reputations as particularly active reformers (e.g., Howell T. Heflin, Sue Bell Cobb, Wallace B. Jefferson, Judith S. Kaye, Mary J. Mullarkey, Edward E. Pringle, Thomas R. Phillips). In several states (Connecticut, Illinois, Mississippi, Tennessee), State of the Judiciary reports were almost entirely informational and seldom asked lawmakers to address court needs via specific actions.

A handful of issues were central for court leaders around the United States, though there are meaningful differences in top concerns among them. Raised most often by court leaders in half of the states were housekeeping issues, individually or tied with another priority. This is consistent with the overall trend in our data. It is interesting, though, that court leaders in the other half of the states focused more on other concerns. In eight states, the most frequent type of request focused on the need for additional judgeships or staff due to excessive workloads. Court leaders in seven states most often requested legislative attention to salaries and benefits, indicating persistent concerns with insufficient compensation. Structural change was given the most attention in four states. Delaware's chief justices focused extensively on court reorganization and jurisdictional change. In Florida, Indiana, and Minnesota, proposals related to structural change were most common in the 1970s and 1980s, while the states' court systems worked toward unification or establishing intermediate appellate courts. Chief justices in a trio of states—Pennsylvania, Texas, and Virginia—most often requested legislative attention to judicial selection. Their requests tended to ask for the state to abandon its method of judicial selection in favor of an alternative. Chiefs in three states devoted the most attention to statutory revisions. In one state, South Dakota, the most common type of request related to budgeting for the judiciary. In State of the Judiciary messages, South Dakota's chief justices frequently stated specific budget needs and requested that legislators refrain from budget cuts.

Conclusion

This chapter demonstrates how modern court leaders use public speeches to advocate for their court systems. As the opening examples illustrate, Chief Justice Rush and Chief Judge DiFiore discussed the accomplishments and deficiencies of their state court systems with the intention of educating others and generating interest in the needs of the judiciary. Our findings indicate that such behavior has become common throughout the United States as judicial leaders have embraced their expanded leadership roles. Many chief justices clearly take their administrative responsibilities seriously. They now act as the primary advocates for their court systems, no longer relying on bar associations and friendly legislators to spearhead reform efforts. The leaders of state court systems can now behave as agenda setters and deliver informative messages supported by the efforts of court administrators.

As a result of engaging with the broader justice system, chief justices have become legitimatized messengers on behalf of state courts and affiliated institutions. Our analysis of their reform agendas indicates that chief justices respond to contemporaneous conditions, recognizing the unique needs of their state courts. We find that chief justices from states that have achieved structural reforms (court unification, creation of intermediate appellate court, and revised jurisdiction) can turn their attention to more mundane issues like institutional upkeep. Meanwhile, chiefs who lead court systems plagued by unmanageable workloads or inadequate judicial compensation often focus on those issues rather than other goals. We also find evidence that court leaders respond to broader trends such as the creation of accountability courts. Where chief justices perceive that initiatives may offer solutions to persistent problems, they tend to add those initiatives to their list of goals.

The evidence also shows that chief justices typically adopt the strategy endorsed by Chief Justice Wathen, focusing their efforts on a small number of goals rather than a long list of proposals. With an average of just two specific proposals that require legislative action, chief justices are not bombarding their partners in the legislative branch with requests. Much like governors and presidents, chief justices construct their agendas carefully to improve their chances of success in the policy arena. Given that court leaders promote issues without a natural constituency beyond lawyers and judges, it is understandable that they refrain from overwhelming policymakers with extensive wish lists.

While chief justices can create agendas, it is apparent that they have less control over opportunities to announce their preferences. Appearances before legislators or bar associations tend to require invitations, and states have developed different norms regarding the frequency and venue of State of the Judiciary remarks. Chief justices also do not control whether their advocacy efforts are taken seriously by state legislatures.

Just as it is important to understand how chief justices act as advocates for state court systems and respond to needs of the judiciary and to the political environment in which it exists, it is important to address the extent to which court leaders get the reforms they have requested from policymakers. A sure sign of contemporary judicial leadership is the chief justice's effectiveness in judicial policy efforts. We take up that topic in the next chapter.

CHAPTER 5

The Chief Justice as Politician

In his January 2019 State of the Judiciary speech to the Texas legislature, Chief Justice Nathan L. Hecht emphasized the problem of low judicial compensation. Judges in his state had only received two pay raises in nearly two decades, and their salaries were 20–30 percent lower than judges received in other states with similar population sizes (Kowalick 2019). A 2018 report of the Texas Judicial Compensation Commission had recommended a pay raise of 15 percent for Texas judges. Hecht emphasized the need for pay raises in three consecutive State of the Judiciary addresses, beginning in 2015. In his 2019 report, Hecht asserted that "public service should not be public servitude" and that "Texas has not compensated her judges fairly" (Hecht 2019). He asked legislators to support pending legislation that would reward prolonged judicial service by providing pay raises. He also appeared before the Appropriations Committee of the Texas House in February 2019, emphasizing the need for higher compensation for judges and staff. In March 2019, David Slayton, administrative director of the Office of Court Administration, appeared before the House Judiciary and Civil Jurisprudence Committee to also make the case for judicial pay raises (Slayton 2019).

Chief Justice Hecht clearly made increasing judicial salaries a high priority in 2019. Further, his strategy of bringing attention and political pressure to the issue used the platform associated with the chief justice position. His State of the Judiciary address was a place for consistent and repeated messaging about the problem. As he began to use stronger and more provocative language about the issue, media coverage extended the urgency of his message to the broader Texas voting public.[1] Finally, he was able to appeal directly to the legislature via his role as chief justice.

Chief Justice Hecht's work to raise awareness of inadequate judicial compensation in Texas was ultimately successful. In June 2019, Texas Governor Greg W. Abbott signed into law a substantial pay raise for many of the state's judges. The Senate's sponsor of the judicial compensation bill, Joan J. Huffman (R-Houston), explained that establishing "longevity pay" for judges would provide a "nice bump to judges who have stuck around and have been doing a great job for us" (Garrett 2019). Its principal House sponsor, Jeff C. Leach (R-Plano), issued a celebratory press release explicitly quoting Chief Justice Hecht's rhetoric about the importance of the bill (Leach 2019).

Hecht's successful political advocacy in Texas serves as a useful illustration. Judges in the Lone Star State coped with unsatisfactory compensation for many years but found legislators disinterested or unable to address the problem, despite several consecutive recommendations for pay hikes from the Texas Judicial Compensation Commission. Chief Justice Hecht made judicial pay raises an administrative priority and ultimately found legislative success in the endeavor. What made it possible for the chief justice to achieve his goal? In this chapter, we explore the conditions that affect the success or failure of chief justices as politicians and advocates for the state court systems. We build on the last chapter's analysis of the reform agendas of chief justices. Our findings reveal that the ideological proximity between chiefs and state legislators, the scope of the policy, the audience receiving the address, the size of the chief justice's agenda, and the beneficiaries of the policy influence whether requests from chief justices are granted by legislators.

Communicating the Reform Agenda

All else equal, judges are at a disadvantage when hoping to improve their courts. Lawmakers often lack interest or knowledge about the needs of the judiciary. The courts do not have a natural constituency that elevates their attractiveness as a focus for lawmakers concerned about reelection and the interests of their home districts. Judicial reform is usually a "low legislative priority" that competes for attention with education, taxation, and other areas of public policy (Glick 1982, 22). In addition, few individuals other than attorneys have frequent interactions with the judiciary.

As a result, judges' job satisfaction and the efficiency of case processing are seldom paramount concerns for typical citizens. Judicial reform can also be disadvantaged by hesitation among judges to engage with politics, a reluctance borne out of traditional, legal, and political realities. Jurists frequently shun activities that politicize the courts or encroach on the prerogatives of lawmakers. The behavior of judges is also limited by canons of judicial conduct that restrict lobbying and advocacy activities (Cannon 1982; Gertner 2004; Hartley 2014). In addition, judges and legislators tend to have different personality types (Cannon 1982), with judges suited more to the formal procedures of a courtroom than to the wheeling and dealing involved in legislative politics.

The chief justice functions as the chief advocate for the state judiciary and can both publicize faults of the justice system and promote possible solutions. As shown in chapter 4, State of the Judiciary messages are frequently used for both purposes. They present chief justices with opportunities to disseminate information about courts to individuals who can encourage change or address court needs directly. The reports announce the reform agenda of the chief justice, backed by the prestige and political clout associated with the position.

Chief justices choose to what degree they wish to spearhead reform efforts. They also choose how much of the work they delegate to others (Tobin 1999, 149). While the chief justice is the primary advocate and political leader for judicial reform, a chief has help with administrative responsibilities and reform efforts. Partners may include the office of the state court administrator, other judges, the organized bar, and (where applicable) the state judicial council. Chief Justice Donald R. Wright of California emphasized his reliance on teamwork to achieve reforms:

> Court reform required a form of tripartite support. First there must be system leadership based on the prestige and stature of the Chief Justices; second, there must be a general willingness to follow that leadership based upon its credibility within the judicial system; finally, there must be a strong judicial management structure comprised of informed policy advisors and a competent staff. (Kleps 1977, 685)

Armed with administrative partners and competent staff, a chief justice can create a State of the Judiciary address that alerts the state legislature about the policy changes needed to improve the state justice system. Rhetoric by chief justices suggests that motivating improvement is precisely their intention. Chief Justice Wallace B. Jefferson of Texas referred to the State of the Judiciary as the way judges have "a voice in the legislature," using it to "highlight pressing judicial issues, while educating the public on recent progress made and lingering obstacles that lie ahead" (Jefferson 2010, 629). In the State of the Judiciary address, a chief justice has a platform to facilitate a top leadership priority: taking care of the state judiciary.

Achieving Judicial Reforms

Of course, asking for judicial improvements does not guarantee policymakers will adopt them. There are several reasons for that political reality. First, judicial requests are considered by legislators already engaged with other policy priorities. Second, legislators are concerned about their own prospects for reelection (Friesen 1977; Mayhew 1974). Many of the alternative priorities considered by legislators provide more opportunities for position taking, credit claiming, and advertising (Mayhew 1974). Finally, the public is often unaware of the problems of the courts and fails to see those problems as high priorities for state governments. Legislators' motivations and their and the public's priorities affect adoption of judicial improvements, given that state court reforms are achieved via political processes rather than through altruism or automatic responses to the decline of court systems (Dubois 1982; Friesen 1977; Gallas 1979; Wilhelm, Vining, Boldt, and Black 2020).

Although chief justices and their allies would likely prefer apolitical evaluation of their requests for judicial reform, that reform agenda often activates political impulses (Gallas 1979). Issues like judicial selection, judicial power, access to courts and attorneys, and resource distribution have clear implications for politics and policy (Douglas and Hartley 2003; Friesen 1977). Courts must request assistance and resources from the same institutions whose actions the courts evaluate and sometimes rebuke. Legislators may not be eager to assist courts or judges if they are perceived as shirking legislative preferences, favoring unpopular social or cultural values, or contributing to social upheaval (Dubois 1982, 1–2; Friesen 1977, 38; Vining, Wilhelm, and Hughes 2019). Given that courts address contentious issues, it is not surprising that judicial policy requests may prompt a political response (Gallas 1979, 37).

Remarks by chief justices suggest that they comprehend the political constraints in which they operate. Chief Justice Leah Ward Sears of Georgia began her 2007 message to the legislature with a brief description of the goals the State of the Judiciary speech was meant to achieve, emphasizing the importance of cordial interbranch relations.

(1) It reminds us of the vital mission of the judicial branch to administer justice under the law equally to all.

(2) It reaffirms our partnership with the legislative and executive branches in identifying and allocating the resources and tools we need to carry out our mission.

(3) It gives us a public opportunity to express the judicial branch's thanks and appreciation for your positive and constructive role in this trilateral partnership.

(4) Finally, it is the best forum I have to share with you and the people of Georgia our assessment of the state's judicial system. (Sears 2007)

Arkansas chief justice James R. (Jim) Hannah began his 2011 State of the Judiciary address with similar sentiments, noting that such remarks "make the point . . . that our constitution has established the judiciary as a co-equal and independent branch of government." Often appearing in speeches by chief justices, such comments offer a hat tip to the state legislature for continued goodwill and remind policymakers about the importance of the legislative-judicial partnership.

Given that judicial reform requests are subject to the same obstacles as other state-level policy initiatives, what do we know about the success of judicial reform efforts? Previous empirical studies have focused primarily on a specific kind of reform initiative, such as judicial selection (Kritzer 2020; Marcin 2015; Tarr 2012) or court funding (Douglas and Hartley 2001, 2003; Hartley and Douglas 2003). These studies are instructive and informative but examine small subsets of potential reforms. We move beyond analyses of specific reform areas and broaden the focus.

For the analysis in this chapter, we are interested in the wide-ranging set of reform efforts in which the chief justice has a primary role via leadership of the state judiciary. The data from State of the Judiciary addresses we analyzed in chapter 4 includes an extensive list of judicial reform requests highlighted by chief justices across states and over time. In this chapter, we evaluate the conditions associated with the success or failure of these reforms promoted by chief justices. Our systematic analysis identifies the forces within the state policymaking environment that chief justices must navigate to achieve their goals as judicial leaders.

Primary Factors Predicting Success

THE STATE POLITICAL ENVIRONMENT AND POLICY SCOPE

Although the traditional view of the judiciary portrays it as apolitical, it is naive to expect that judicial reforms are evaluated without political considerations (Glick 1981). State legislators know well that courts and judges issue rulings with legal and political consequences. Further, the process to enact reforms via legislation or constitutional amendments is inherently political. Even when viewed favorably by policymakers, proposals for judicial reform are subject to the multistage lawmaking process affected by competing priorities, limited resources, and finite legislative time. The enactment of items on the judicial reform agenda is likely facilitated by cordial relations between the branches of government and by sociopolitical conditions associated with legislative efficiency and budget flexibility.

A basic understanding of the state policy environment suggests that a chief justice's policy requests are more likely to receive favorable treatment when relations between the judicial and legislative branches are congenial rather than combative. In other words, lawmakers are more likely to grant a court leader's requests for judicial reform when the judiciary is perceived as "friendly." Given that legislators tend to seek public office to advance their own policy priorities, they are more likely to support chief justices (and their courts) that help in that regard.

Public actions and remarks by judicial leaders suggest that interbranch relations are a major influence on judicial reform. For example, in a 2005 State of the Judiciary message, Chief Justice Daniel E. Wathen of Maine argued that cordial judicial-legislative relations are important when a chief justice requests adequate budgetary support for state courts (Wathen 2005). In a 2007 State of the Judiciary address, Chief Justice Ronald T. Y. Moon of Hawaii commented, "There is no doubt that we— that is, all three branches of government—are well aware that we share in the quest for fairness, justice, and good government as we work both collaboratively and separately to serve the people of Hawai'i." Similar remarks are common in chief justices' public pronouncements. That the improvement of interbranch relations and communications has been a persistent theme of judges' professional conferences for decades (see, e.g., Christie and Maron 1991) demonstrates that judicial actors understand the consequences of legislative-judicial relations.

If the judicial branch is at odds with the state legislature, it is likely to have consequences for policies related to the judiciary. Consider, for example, the treatment of courts in Iowa following the state supreme court's unanimous *Varnum v. Brien*[2] decision that legalized same-sex marriage in the state. Three justices on the Iowa Supreme Court—David L. Baker, Michael J. Streit, and Chief Justice Marsha K. Ternus—were rejected in their 2010 retention elections after a massive campaign against them. Additionally, the Iowa state legislature introduced initiatives that included the mass impeachment of the remaining justices. When Chief Justice Mark S. Cady appeared before the Iowa legislature in 2011, he requested more court funding, but most of his remarks were devoted to defending the role of independent courts rather than to promoting a package of judicial improvements (Volsky 2011). The state legislature responded with no substantial budget increase, which meant that Iowa courts had to carry on with staffing levels lower than in 1987 while district court filings had increased by 66 percent (Bluestein 2011). Policymakers refused to improve the condition of the justice system and simultaneously attacked the judiciary with court-curbing legislation.

The aforementioned events in Iowa were highly publicized and controversial. However, we expect that legislative support for judicial reforms is conditional even when the courts are not involved in highly visible interbranch disputes. State legislators looking for political alliances are likely to be aware of the ideological tendencies of a state's chief justice and court of last resort. Because the chief justice is the main political representative of the state judiciary, we anticipate that legislators associate items on the judicial reform agenda with the leader of the court system. As a result, we expect that the ideological leanings of the chief justice will influence the response of legislators to reform proposals.

PREDICTION 1: *A chief justice's reform request has a greater likelihood of enactment when legislative-judicial ideological distance is lower.*

Similar to their effects on other legislation, several aspects of the state political environment are likely to influence the success of judicial reform proposals. For example, the presence of unified or divided state government has a significant impact on the policy process (Bowling and Ferguson 2001). During unified government, there is a higher likelihood that state political leaders will agree about goals and how to achieve them. In periods of divided government, disagreement that hinders a state government's efficiency in policymaking is more likely. We anticipate that the same dynamics will be present when legislators and governors consider whether to adopt judicial reforms.

PREDICTION 2: *A chief justice's reform request has a greater likelihood of enactment during periods of unified state government.*

THE SCOPE OF THE POLICY REQUEST

Along with the political environment, we expect that the other major factor driving the success or failure of reform efforts is the scope of a request. Simply put, legislators are more likely to enact minor judicial reforms than major changes. Incremental changes result in less disruption to the status quo, which limits their significance. They also tend to cost less money to implement than major reforms (Eshbaugh-Soha 2010). Scholars of judicial administration have acknowledged the effect of policy scope (Sherman 1977; Glick 1982, 1983) without providing an empirical test of its impact. Glick (1982) contended that the success of a judicial reform effort depends partially on what it will accomplish and how it will affect local control of courts. He also argued that "the less change a reform required and the fewer judges and other personnel it affects, the more likely it is to be adopted" (Glick 1983, 63). Sherman (1977, 68–69) invoked the limitations imposed by costs: "Perhaps the greatest problem to overcome in the quest for court reform is the high cost associated with the changes advocated."

As we discussed in chapter 4, there is substantial variation in the scope of judicial reforms that chief justices request. Routine requests for institutional upkeep, budget increases to match inflation, or marginal staff increases are less likely to have political consequences or to activate partisan instincts in state legislators than are reforms that tilt the balance of political power or affect partisan goals. Sweeping changes to judicial selection or the reorganization of state court systems, for example, are more likely to be perceived as politically significant than is routine maintenance of the judiciary.

Similar considerations influence the passage of agenda items requested by American presidents. Accordingly, Eshbaugh-Soha (2010) developed a dichotomous measure of important and routine agenda items to classify requests made in presidential speeches. He used that framework to evaluate the impact of policy scope on the likelihood of presidential success. The framework is transportable to the context of judicial reform requests promoted by chief justices, which also vary widely in terms of their impact and costs (Vining, Wilhelm, and Hughes 2019; Wilhelm, Vining, Boldt, and Black 2020).

In our analysis, we designated agenda items as important if they would have major, long-term effects on the justice system. These items include proposals to create or eliminate a judicial body, alter materially the relationship between state citizens and the judicial system, or increase substantially the number of judgeships on a given state court. We classify requests for judgeships as important if the number requested is equal to or greater than 10 percent of the existing number of judges on a given state court. Such events are rare, with chief justices typically requesting new judgeships singularly rather than in bundles. Important proposals also include those that broadly affect access to justice or that would reform a state's judicial selection system. Requests that improve the salaries, benefits, or working conditions of individual judges are classified as routine rather than important, as they have a limited impact on the American people. Based on our classification method, 14 percent of requests are labeled as important agenda items. We expect less likelihood of enactment for those items than for routine ones.

PREDICTION 3: *Important requests have a decreased likelihood of enactment relative to routine requests.*

Other Factors Predicting Policy Success

Along with interbranch relations and the scope of the reform request, other factors likely influence the success (or failure) of court leaders' requests for judicial reform. We group these factors as related to the chief justice, the relevant judicial address, the state judiciary, the state legislature, and the economy.

FACTORS RELATED TO THE CHIEF JUSTICE

The chief justice is most directly associated with the agenda for judicial reform and serves as the judiciary's primary liaison to the legislature. It stands to reason that a chief justice's personal characteristics might impact how a state legislature relates to a reform requested by the chief.

Although we cannot directly measure each chief justice's ambition toward reform or "likeability" among policymakers, we can analyze the impact of differences among chief justices that may temper their success in the policy arena.

First, we considered the possibility that a chief justice's gender will influence the success of judicial reform efforts. In the modern era, it has been common for both men and women to serve as chief justices (see chapter 2). Scholars have given significant attention to whether male and female chief justices run their courts in the same fashion or with similar effectiveness (Kaye 2005; Leonard and Ross 2020). Norris and Whittington (2018) found meaningful differences in how male and female judges in state supreme courts expect chief justices to behave. However, we have little understanding of whether gender differences in judicial branch leadership yield different outcomes in court reform or interbranch relations. Here, we consider whether men and women differ in their abilities to navigate the policymaking process associated with judicial reforms. Approximately 30 percent of the policy items we analyze were proposed by women chief justices.

Second, we consider how variation in the tenure of chief justices affects their ability to achieve their reform goals. Some selection systems (e.g., rotation) lend themselves to shorter tenures, while others (seniority and popular election) facilitate longer periods as chief justices. We speculate that no matter how they acquired the position, junior chief justices may come with reform goals they pursue aggressively early in their tenures. Senior chief justices may be more skilled in terms of guiding their reform requests to legislative enactment. During the time period analyzed here, the experience of chief justices ranged from freshmen to 24 years, with approximately 60 percent of proposals coming from chief justices with five or less years of experience.

Finally, we consider how methods of chief justice selection affect reform success. As discussed in chapter 1, the selection methods differ across states. Some high court judges ascend to the chief justiceship via seniority or rotation, while others are chosen by peer vote or a popular election. Chief justices who acquired the position in a popular election are uniquely able to assert a popular mandate for their reform agendas. However, their counterparts chosen by other means may be most capable of claiming the support of politicians or of their supreme court colleagues, depending on the method of selection.

FACTORS RELATED TO THE STATE OF
THE JUDICIARY ADDRESS

The success of the chief justice's policy agenda may also be related to the venue of a State of the Judiciary address. Remarks given directly to lawmakers likely have the greatest impact, while written reports or talks given to other audiences (e.g., state bar meetings) may not pack the same punch. When a chief justice is afforded the captive attention of the state legislature, he commands the notice of the individuals who will craft or approve the policies requested. No other audience creates that direct-to-source engagement. During the time period analyzed, 79 percent of proposals were delivered directly to state legislatures.

Another aspect of the judicial address that may factor into policy success is the number of reform proposals competing for legislative attention. Chief justices who limit agendas to a small number of proposals emphasize the importance of those requests and give legislators clear direction regarding their highest priorities. As a chief justice's reform agenda grows in size, proposals increasingly compete for legislative time and attention. The result may be inaction even where the chief justice does not face specific opposition. In the time period analyzed here, the number of reform requests in a chief justice's message varied from 1 to 22.[3] Most reports (around 80 percent) included 6 reform proposals or fewer.

FACTORS RELATED TO THE STATE JUDICIARY

As discussed in chapter 1, there are differences in institutional arrangements across state judiciaries. It is possible that these differences influence whether judicial reforms are adopted. One difference we consider is the selection method of the state supreme court. Appointed judges have clear connections to the political institutions that pick them for their jobs, which may yield an advantage when seeking court improvements. On the other hand, elected judges can claim a popular mandate that is not associated with appointed jurists. These differences may affect the success of a chief justice asking for judicial reforms.

Another difference we consider is the range of professionalism among state high courts. The professionalism of a state supreme court is related to its judicial salaries, docket control, and staff resources (Squire 2008; Squire and Butcher 2021). There is substantial variation among state courts in this regard, with some courts highly professionalized (e.g., California, Michigan, and Pennsylvania) and others less so (e.g., North Dakota, South Dakota, and Vermont). State legislators may respond to the relative strengths and shortcomings of their state courts, at least when they are aware of them.

FACTORS RELATED TO THE STATE LEGISLATURE

Factors related to the state legislature and its goals may also influence the adoption of the chief justice's requested reforms. One key institutional difference among states is the professionalism of the state legislature (Squire 2008). Legislatures with a higher level of professionalism may deliberate more thoroughly when developing policy and may have more sustained relations with the other branches of government (Rosenthal 1998). They are also likely to be more skilled at policy implementation (Karnig and Siegelman 1975; Roeder 1979). These traits give a legislature that is more professionalized a greater investment and interest in the functions of the state's judicial branch, which may facilitate the adoption of judicial reforms.

A second factor relates more directly to the goals of legislators. State policymakers are likely to consider the intended recipients of the reforms urged by chief justices. In other words, a legislator may consider who the policy benefits and whether this can have electoral consequences. Many initiatives advanced by judicial leaders seek assistance for marginalized or underrepresented groups in American society, including prisoners, racial minorities, disabled citizens, children, and individuals of limited financial means (Wilhelm, Vining, Boldt, and Black 2020). Advocacy of this type is consistent with the role of chief justices as justice leaders (Raftery 2017). However, these populations are less likely to be engaged with the political process as voters or donors whose support would benefit state legislators (Smets and van Ham 2013). Nonetheless, chief justices have the ability to draw attention to systemic deficiencies affecting underrepresented groups in the justice system and to generate public or legislative support for reform. To determine whether legislatures evaluate reform proposals differently depending on the marginalization of the group represented, we control for policies that benefit underrepresented groups. In the time period analyzed, 11 percent of all requests were in this category.

FACTORS RELATED TO THE STATE ECONOMY

The last factor we consider is the state's economic condition, which undoubtedly structures the policymaking environment. Legislators may be more likely to approve judicial reforms when the state economy and state finances are robust. Legislators are sensitive to the costs of potential reforms during periods of economic instability or recession when other priorities compete with the judiciary for tax dollars (Sherman 1977). When the state's economy is healthy, legislators can turn their attention to lingering topics like the judiciary rather than focusing on pressing matters generated by economic decline, widespread unemployment, or maintaining a balanced budget.

Data, Analysis, and Results

To examine factors that influence the likelihood of enactment for a chief justice's requests for judicial maintenance or improvements, we examined the legislative success of items on the chief justice's agenda from 1990 to 2020.[4] In this 30-year period, 1,376 items were requested by chief justices in their State of the Judiciary addresses. Due to missing data in a subset of our observations, our analysis was limited to 1,220 requests. To determine whether a request was enacted, we reviewed subsequent judicial reports, Westlaw's database of state legislative activity (BILLTRK and BILLTRK-OLD),[5] the legislative database maintained by the National Center for State Courts,[6] and individual state websites tracking legislative activity. A court leader's request was considered "enacted" if state policymakers responded with corresponding legislation or appropriations (as relevant) prior to the delivery of the next State of the Judiciary report. In total, 39 percent of all requests in our data were enacted by state legislatures.

Summary statistics describing our dependent variable and the variables used in our model are described in table 5.1. Given their compatibility, we measured ideological distance using updated versions of Brace, Langer, and Hall's (2000) scores of party-adjusted judge ideology (PAJID) and the governmental ideology scores used by Berry, et al. (2013). Calculating ideological distance as the absolute value of the difference between institutions indicated the relative magnitude of their disagreement. All other variable measurements and sources are noted in the summary table.

Table 5.1. Model Summary Statistics

	Mean (s.d.)	Range	Data source
Dependent Variable			
Request granted	0.39 (0.49)	0–1	Computed by this study's authors
Independent Variables			
Chief Justice-legislative ideological distance	24.1 (13.7)	0–63.4	Brace, Langer, and Hall 2000; Hughes and Wilhelm 2021; Berry et al. 1998 (updated)
Unified government	0.46 (0.50)	0–1	National Conference for State Legislatures
Important request	0.14 (0.34)	0–1	Computed by this study's authors
Female chief justice	0.31 (0.46)	0–1	Goelzhauser 2016 (updated)
Chief justice tenure	5.95 (4.73)	0–24	Computed by this study's authors
Elected chief justice	0.12 (0.32)	0–1	Council of State Governments 2020
Legislative audience	0.79 (0.41)	0–1	Computed by this study's authors
Total proposals	4.80 (3.73)	1–22	Computed by this study's authors
Elected court	0.30 (0.46)	0–1	Council of State Governments 2020
Court professionalization	0.59 (0.17)	0.25–1.08	Squire and Butcher 2021
Legislative professionalization	0.21 (0.15)	0.03–0.65	Squire 2007
Underrepresented group issue	0.11 (0.31)	0–1	Computed by this study's authors
Gross state product per capita (thousands of dollars)	43.29 (11.92)	18.62–79.83	Bureau of Economic Analysis 2022, Census Bureau 2021

Note: N = 1,220 observations. Chief justice tenure = 0 if a chief justice is in the first year of leadership.

We analyzed the likelihood that a chief justice's request will be enacted (1) or not (0). Given the binary nature of our dependent variable, we used logistic regression. To account for variation among the states, we used clustered robust standard errors. We also controlled for differences over time by including fixed effects for the year of the address. The results of our analysis are presented in table 5.2. We report changes in predicted probability for all variables that reach statistical significance.

Our model estimates support the idea that the political environment influences the success of court leaders' requests for judicial improvements. The greater the ideological distance between the chief justice and state policymakers, the less likely a given agenda item will be adopted ($p < 0.05$, one-tailed test). In figure 7, we display the predicted probability that a request is granted over the range of the ideological distance measure with all other variables held at mean values (for continuous variables) or modal values (for binary variables).

The predicted probability that a request is granted decreases from 48 percent to 36 percent as ideological proximity shifts from the most proximate to the most distant chief justices. This finding emphasizes

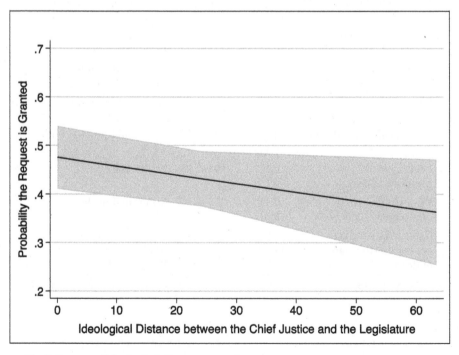

Fig. 7. Impact of ideological distance on policy success

Table 5.2. Logistic Regression Results for Judicial Requests Granted by the State Legislature

Variable	Coefficient (Std. error)	Change in predicted probability (at min, at max.)
Chief Justice-legislative ideological distance	**-0.01*** **(0.00)**	0.48, 0.36
Unified government	0.12 (0.13)	
Important request	**-0.73^** **(0.27)**	0.43, 0.28
Female chief justice	-0.15 (0.18)	
Chief justice tenure	-0.01 (0.01)	
Elected chief justice	-0.18 (0.19)	
Legislative audience	**1.07^** **(0.21)**	0.22, 0.43
Total proposals	**-0.05^** **(0.02)**	0.48, 0.25
Elected court	0.17 (0.14)	
Court professionalization	0.51 (0.54)	
Legislative professionalization	0.79 (0.86)	
Underrepresented group issue	**0.94^** **(0.21)**	0.43, 0.65
Gross state product per capita (thousands of dollars)	0.01 (0.01)	
Constant	-0.87 (0.81)	
N	1,215	
Bayesian information criterion	1756.45	
Percent reduction in error	16.11%	

Note: The logistic regression model includes fixed effects for year and standard errors clustered by state. Changes in predicted probabilities calculated from minimum to maximum values for continuous variables and 0 to 1 for dichotomous variables.

the importance of shared political leanings between a chief justice and state legislature to accomplish judicial policy needs. Although courts are often characterized as existing outside the political realm, the process for maintaining the state judiciary is entangled with political considerations.

Contrary to most studies of policymaking, we do not find evidence that unified or divided government in the state affects the likelihood that a judicial request will be enacted, which suggests that issues surrounding the justice system are treated differently than other categories of legislation. What we do find, however, is that the scope of the policy request promoted by the chief justice has a significant impact on its likelihood of success ($p < 0.01$). Important requests, those having the most impact on the justice system, have a 0.28 predicted probability of enactment versus a 0.43 probability for routine requests. This difference reflects the usual pattern in policymaking, with major reforms being more difficult to achieve than changes at the margins. Our results regarding ideological proximity and the scope of policy requests support two of our three key predictions, indicating that political considerations and policy scope are important determinants of success for chief justices when they engage with the legislative process.

The analysis of our control variables indicates that both institutional variation and chief justices' characteristics influence whether agenda items are enacted. Delivering the address directly to the legislature has a profound impact on the likelihood of enactment ($p < 0.001$). All else being equal, a request delivered orally to the state legislature had a predicted enactment probability of roughly 0.43. When the chief justice made the request to another audience, the predicted probability dropped to just 0.22. That drop is to be expected because legislators may not be aware of needs that were not articulated in their presence. Given the meaningful impact of the delivery variable, one can understand why many chief justices seek invitations to statehouses or become frustrated when such opportunities are denied or withdrawn.

Our estimates also suggest that a state's selection method for court leaders does not influence the likelihood of adopting requests for judicial reform. All else being equal, neither popular election nor appointment provides chief justices with a stronger hand in their administrative roles. Neither state court professionalism nor state legislative professionalism has a significant impact on the likelihood of policy success, possibly due to the model's inclusion of state and year fixed effects.

Neither the gender nor the tenure of a chief justice has a significant impact on the likelihood of a request being granted. However, the nature of the request does have an impact. In our analysis, requests designed to aid underrepresented constituent groups were more likely to be adopted than other agenda items ($p < 0.001$). While all other requests had a 0.43 predicted probability of positive treatment, those made on behalf of underrepresented groups had a predicted probability of approximately 0.65. That probability increase may indicate the high value that chief justices place on agenda items concerned with access and equality within their court systems. Furthermore, such social policies may advantage lawmakers in terms of their electoral security.

Not surprisingly, we found that more total requests in an address are associated with a lower probability of enactment ($p < 0.01$). Accordingly, presenting a narrow set of requests serves chief justices better than offering a long list of agenda items.

Conclusion

In this chapter, we considered the function of the chief justice as political leader for the state judiciary. For the judicial branch to function, it depends on a state legislature with limited resources and competing priorities. The chief justice must navigate this policymaking environment to secure the needs of courts and judges. Examining the chief justice's most visible advocacy efforts reveals the importance of the political environment in these endeavors. Specifically, we found that ideological proximity between the chief justice and state policymakers influences the likelihood that the chief justice will achieve improvements for the judiciary. We also found that the scope of the chief justice's request matters. Routine requests are more likely to be granted than those with higher stakes. Contextual factors matter as well, with legislators responding to the health of the state economy and the crowdedness of the chief justice's agenda.

Our findings emphasize the importance of the chief justice as an administrative leader, as well as the relevance of state politics for court reform. The opening example in this chapter provides a tangible illustration of our findings. Most obvious about Chief Justice Hecht's requests for salary increases from the Texas legislature is the importance of political conditions for policy success. Hecht benefited from his Republican Party affiliation and conservative leanings given the state's GOP leadership. Most Texas legislators would have little reason to perceive the chief justice or his court as hostile adversaries. The scope of Hecht's request was also modest relative to the broader state budget. His proposed reform was reasonably affordable given its impact of approximately $34 million every two years in a biennial budget of $250 billion. He also concentrated on his efforts for salary increases, with a repetitive and narrow focus. Finally, that he or his representative appeared in person to make direct appeals to the Texas legislature likely placed the issue on the radar of policymakers who were not aware of the extent of the problem or its possible repercussions.

Overall, our model estimates support our general argument that court leaders must carry out their administrative responsibilities within the constraints of their political environments. Although judicial reform is often framed in apolitical terms by judges and their allies, chief justices are decidedly more successful when asking their ideological kin for assistance. This is consistent with arguments offered by Glick (1981) and other midcentury scholars of judicial administration who asserted that court reform should be viewed as intersecting with ordinary politics. That wave of judicial reform studies rarely included rigorous empirical analyses to test their claims. Here and in our earlier research on federal and state courts (Vining, Wilhelm, and Hughes 2019; Wilhelm, Vining, Boldt, and Black 2020), we have consistently found that the success of court reform efforts is conditioned by interbranch relations and policy scope. It is apparent that court leaders who wish to find legislative success for their reform priorities should be aware of their political environment, the scope of their requests, the audience to which they present requests, and the size of their agenda. Chief justices' rhetoric about State of the Judiciary reports often expresses intuition consistent with the results of our analysis. Strategic court leaders may be well advised to take advantage of conditions that make successful reforms more likely, particularly when reaching beyond incremental changes.

Conclusion

In January 2003, Montana Chief Justice Karla M. Gray became aware that the state legislature was developing a proposal that would send juveniles directly into the adult probation system in the event of certain crimes. Gray, an outspoken advocate for youth rights in the criminal justice system, was immediately alarmed by the possibility. She called an urgent press conference to denounce the legislation, during which she announced stern opposition to the bill.

> This will be a might battle. But I will not jeopardize Montana's kids by waiting to battle under the timeline arranged by the powers behind this bill; I will not wait until this bill is introduced . . . and be trapped into someone else's timing for a hearing. This is far too important for that. (Gouras 2003)

As the first female chief justice in Montana, Gray had a long and storied career in state politics. Perhaps most important, she was known as a tireless advocate for equality in Montana's justice system. She also had a reputation as someone who was not afraid to speak her mind.

After Gray's concerns were made public and she repeated them at additional events (McKee 2003), the bill that she condemned was not enacted. In fact, the bill was not even introduced into the Montana state legislature that year. Based on the facts presented in news coverage, we cannot conclusively say that Chief Justice Gray preempted the Montana

131

legislature from policy action. However, if we consider the circumstances of her actions alongside the research presented in this book, we think a strong case can be made that her actions deterred the legislation.

The present monograph demonstrates several concepts that are relevant to that episode. Summarily, Chief Justice Gray acted as administrative head of the justice system rather than restricting her leadership to the state high court. She made a proactive effort to use the prestige of her position to publicize her views on what she saw as wrongheaded legislation that could harm the state's young people, and she did so entirely outside the constraints of a legal opinion. In addition, Gray was perceived as a right-leaning jurist, while Republicans controlled both the statehouse and the governor's mansion. Her words likely carried more political heft with state policymakers under these conditions. Ultimately, the anecdote suggests that Gray affected the state policymaking environment in a manner that social scientists have rarely considered for the state chief justice.

Summary of Findings

In the previous chapters, we presented research based on the fundamental premise that the role of the chief justice in the state political environment cannot fully be understood without acknowledging the administrative significance of the position. Judicial reforms in the 20th century empowered nearly every state's chief justice to be the head or co-leader of the state judiciary. As that empowerment happened, chief justices became more involved in administrative leadership. That shift in chief justice responsibilities has been consequential. The days of a chief justice's activities being limited to intracourt leadership and ceremonial events have passed. What does this change mean for our understanding of the function of the chief justice position in the American states? Our analysis leads to several conclusions.

First, our research clarifies that the modern chief justice functions as an administrative leader as much as anything else. This function reflects an intentional delegation of responsibility, as leadership of the entire state judicial system is allocated to the chief justice in all 50 states, either alone or as head of the state supreme court or judicial council. A shift in chief justice duties proliferated in the 1960s and 1970s and is now dominant throughout the United States. In the modern era, a chief justice is likely to spend as much time (if not more) on managing the state judiciary as on case processing and opinion writing. Court leaders are typically assisted in their activities by a court administrator and associated staff involved in long-term planning and projects, data collection, and oversight of the court system's day-to-day activities. The type of judicial branch management that reformers sought in order to improve the condition and efficiency of court systems has largely been realized. Of course, there remains meaningful variation among court leaders in the constraints that they face in their administrative functions, including both institutional factors (methods of selection, tenure rules, and court administration infrastructure) and political factors (interbranch relations).

Second, our research reveals that the rules of chief justice selection can affect the kinds of chief justices that a state will have, in terms of both ideology and diversity of individuals. Ceteris paribus, we find that states that pick chief justices via popular elections or government appointments (absent a commission) tend to have more conservative court leaders. This result is reached even after controlling for state-specific effects, citizen ideology, and elite ideology. Interestingly, we do not find evidence that any type of chief justice selection method is especially effective at reducing the ideological distance between the appointing authority and the chosen court leader. More than other selection methods, peer vote systems are more closely associated with the selection of diverse court leaders. That association is likely related to frequent leadership turnover in many states and to internal norms emphasizing seniority or equity. In addition, members of the high court may be more comfortable than voters, politicians, or commissioners with elevating a candidate who does not conform to a "traditional" model, since coworkers would have spent years observing their colleague's work ethic, abilities, and temperament.

Finally, we find that chief justices can accomplish institutional improvements for the state judiciary if they prioritize them and if statewide political conditions are right. Our historical analysis reveals substantial variation in the advocacy activities of chief justices. However, when court leaders present an agenda for judicial reform and promote it, they can be quite successful. Court leaders generally find the most success for their reform proposals when they share ideological congruence with other political leaders in the state. Beyond a "friendly" policymaking environment, the scope of a chief justice's policy can also impact whether state legislators will adopt a proposal. Reform attempts with the greatest impact or cost are less likely to be enacted, while incremental changes receive more favorable treatment from lawmakers. Each of our results is consistent with previous research examining federal and state judicial reform efforts (Hughes, Vining, and Wilhelm 2017; Vining, Wilhelm, and Hughes 2019; Wilhelm, Vining, Boldt, and Black 2020), providing further evidence that advocacy efforts made by chief justices on behalf of state judiciaries are politicized much like the policy agendas of other government elites.

Implications

What do our study's findings mean for a broader understanding of political institutions in the American states? The first takeaway is that rules of institutional design matter. Legal and constitutional guidelines shape many aspects of court leadership, from the designated responsibilities of the chief justice position to selection mechanisms and tenure provisions. Changing the rules has profound consequences for jurists and their courts. To that point, consider rules about chief justice selection. States empower judges, the public, governors, legislators, or commissions to select judicial leaders. In a handful of states, leaders of the judicial system are elevated due to their seniority, regardless of their preferences or acumen. While we find that none of the selection systems ensures that the chief justice will be closer ideologically to the appointing authority, we also find evidence that rules about selection can encourage or discourage overall diversity in the kinds of individuals who will serve in the position. Rules about tenure served by chief justices also have consequences. Longer terms provide more opportunity for chief justices to implement a reform program. Shorter terms permit a broader set of individuals to bring perspectives and interests to the court's center seat. Finally, states can empower or handicap maintenance of the state judiciary by virtue of the institutional arrangement of chief justice responsibilities. The justice system depends on other actors in state government to assure its well-being, and the capabilities of judicial administrators are limited by the authority policymakers delegate to those administrators and by the resources at the administrators' disposal.

Another takeaway is that characteristics of the individuals who occupy judicial leadership positions matter. People who serve as chief justice can be either aggressive or passive in leadership style. They also may be more or less skilled at fostering coalitions to support court improvements. Each chief justice decides what agenda items to promote, the scope of the desired reforms, and how to engage with legislators. Some chiefs are notable for the outsized effort they put into administrative leadership, while some are decidedly not. In addition, judicial leaders have professional experiences and/or backgrounds that influence the kind of chief justice they become. Interestingly, there has been a sharp decline in recent decades in the number of chief justices who came from the highest levels of state politics aside from the office of attorney general. The modern chief justice is more likely to be a career jurist, which suggests state courts have become more well-bounded (Polsby 1968) and professionalized (Squire 2008) than in earlier eras. Another significant change is the gradual growth in numbers of diverse chief justices in recent decades. Women are much more common occupants in the chief justice seat in the modern era. While states with substantial minority populations were home to many of the trailblazing "firsts" among court leaders, minority chief justices are no longer unusual—though they are still not common.

Our final takeaway is that politics matter in leading the judiciary. Although judges might prefer to be treated and viewed in apolitical terms, we find that state court leaders are cognizant of their political environments and that their requests for court reforms are treated more favorably by their ideological allies. For better or worse, the success rate of judicial leaders is partially dependent on political concordance with state legislators. Although judicial administration is seldom examined by political scientists, it activates partisanship in ways analogous to other areas of public policy. Even chief justices and court administrators who wish to fix legitimate, ongoing problems with state justice systems must navigate policymaking environments where judicial requests compete for agenda space and need support from lawmakers focused on other goals (including reelection). Judicial leaders have incentives to be mindful of their place in state politics and to adjust their expectations and efforts accordingly.

Final Thoughts

We were surprised when our research on chief justices led us to focus intently on the importance of the administrative side of the position. As we worked to clarify the political significance of the chief justice role, we realized that we needed to examine chief justice activities outside the high court rather than within it. It occurred to us how woefully understudied this aspect of court leadership truly was, particularly by social scientists. While analysts of public administration devoted a great deal of attention to judicial administration in the 1970s and 1980s, their studies declined in number after many key goals of the movements for court unification and centralization were achieved. Our research intention for this study was to collect and present a body of evidence to demonstrate how judicial leaders remain important in state politics. The central roles they now have in judicial administration, interbranch relations, and public relations have meaningful consequences for citizens, government officials, and state justice systems.

Whether they like it or not, our research shows that chief justices are tied to state politics. Many court leaders possibly understand that they must be mindful of political considerations if they want to foster inter-branch comity, highlight and fix courts' problems, or (in some states) prolong their careers. It is interesting that the roles and profiles of chief justices have changed simultaneously. Occupants of the chief justice office behave and look differently today than half a century ago and now work within institutional settings that provide support and guidance as they lead state courts. The differences among modern state chiefs invite assessments of ideology, diversity, and their effects, aspects we cannot yet study among leaders of the U.S. Supreme Court. Variation in advocacy and communication strategies also help us assess how chief justices can be most effective as leaders. In some instances, that assessment means empirically testing the notions that chief justices have held for decades. For example, analysis of reform success shows that chief justices are more effective advocates when they can address an audience of legislators rather than other spectators. Many court leaders sought opportunities to do so, and we find that their intuition about audience effect was correct.

We hope that the research presented in this study helps to shape the overall understanding of judicial leadership. It adds to the broader conversation that has primarily focused on intracourt responsibilities of the chief justices rather than on judicial administration. We have not addressed some aspects of administrative leadership in great depth here, including the effect of judicial outreach to citizens and the press, as well as the actual impact of court reforms. We have also given slight attention to how organizations like the Conference of Chief Justices, the National Center for State Courts, and bar groups partner with judicial leaders and assist reform efforts. We perceive those gaps in our analysis as opportunities for future studies, as social scientists continue to examine the chief justices.

Notes

Introduction

1. Moore received widespread national attention during the 2017 U.S. Senate special election in Alabama, as the Republican nominee who was accused of pursuing and dating teenagers while he was in his thirties. His loss to Democratic candidate Doug Jones resulted in the first Democrat-held Senate seat in Alabama in 25 years. Moore's brand of right-wing conservativism is reflected in a history of public statements about race, religion, gender, and views on sexual orientation (Associated Press 2017; Koplowitz 2017; Sullum 2017; Taylor 2017).

2. State courts processed roughly 84.1 million incoming cases in 2018. From March 2018 to March 2019, approximately 1.2 million cases were filed in federal courts. Caseload data available from the Court Statistics Project (2020) by the National Center for State Courts and from the Federal Judicial Caseload statistics compiled by the Administrative Office of the U.S. Courts (2019).

3. Caseload data available from the Court Statistics Project (2020).

4. Data available from Council of State Governments 2021. The shortest state constitution is currently Vermont's (8,565 words), and the longest is Alabama's (nearing 403,000 words).

5. Danelski noted that both these leadership roles can be filled by the chief justice but may be delegated to colleagues. For example, Chief Justice William H. Taft was the social leader of his Court but left the task leadership up to Associate Justice Willis Van Devanter. Chief Justice Charles E. Hughes exhibited both task and social leadership on his court.

6. Raftery (2017) identified Maine and Mississippi as exceptions to this norm, stating that the chief justice is designated as head of the state judiciary by constitution or statute in only 48 of 50 states. However, the Constitution of the State of Maine says, "The Chief Justice is head of the judicial branch," and it names several administrative duties associated with the office (tit. 4, ch. 1, subch. 1). The Mississippi Code specifies the chief justice as "the chief administrative officer of all courts of this state" (Miss. Code § 9-21-3).

Chapter 1

1. The former chief judge, Solomon "Sol" Wachtler, resigned due to a blackmail scandal targeting his former mistress (Mouat 1992).

2. As is common in the literature, we use the phrase "state court of last resort" interchangeably with "state supreme court" or "state high court."

3. In Oklahoma and Texas, state law specifies that administrative leadership of the judicial branch is assigned to the state supreme court and chief justice rather than to the presiding judge of the court of criminal appeals. See Okla. Const. sec. VII-6; Tex. Gov't Code tit. 2, ch. 74, sec. 74.021.

4. President Dwight D. Eisenhower, for example, referred to Earl Warren's appointment to chief justice as "the biggest damn fool mistake I ever made in my life" (Mason 1974, 28).

5. MacDonald founded the New Hampshire chapter of the Federalist Society, a prominent conservative legal organization (Rogers and Ganley 2021).

6. Judicial departures prior to the expiration of a justice's current term are very common in Minnesota due to mandatory retirement at 70 years of age for the state's judges (Magnuson 2020).

7. Weygandt, a Democrat, was seeking his sixth term when he was defeated by Taft, his Republican challenger. Taft's margin of victory was 1,775 votes out of 2,663,007 tabulated statewide.

8. This change happened when Patrick L. McCrory, a Republican governor who had recently lost his 2016 bid for reelection, signed a bill passed in a special session of the state legislature with nearly universal Republican support and Democratic opposition. November 2020 election ballots in North Carolina clearly identified Democratic and Republican candidates for the chief justice position. The chief justice contest featured Senior Associate Justice Paul M. Newby and incumbent Cheri L. Beasley, an African American woman elevated to the position in 2019 by Roy A. Cooper III's gubernatorial appointment.

The Newby-Beasley election was infused with politics due to earlier controversy regarding Beasley's appointment. Governor Cooper had passed over Newby, a Republican, when the chief justice position was vacated. Many Republicans in the state argued that Cooper should have promoted the longest serving justice, Newby, out of political tradition. Newby's electoral challenge to Beasley was ultimately successful. In a year when Republicans won the state's races for the presidency, the U.S. Senate, and both chambers of the state legislature, Newby defeated Beasley by 401 votes out of 5.4 million cast, despite more than a month of legal challenges and recounts (Robertson 2020).

9. The state's chief justices had been designated by seniority since 1889 (D. Hall 2013; Marley 2015).

10. See https://www.leg.state.nv.us/courtrules/scr.html for the Nevada Supreme Court rules.

11. When multiple justices have the same level of seniority, the court's senior justices occasionally divide the term of the chief position among themselves. Senior justices with equal claim to the chief position became relatively common as the court increased in size from three justices to five (in 1967) and then from five members to seven (in 1999) in response to growing caseloads (Sweet 2016, 242). Arrangements to share a term have been used in Nevada since at least 1996, when justices Miriam M. Shearing and Charles E. Springer agreed to split the two-year term (Shearing lead-

ing in 1997, Springer in 1998) rather than flip a coin to select a chief ("Shearing to Lead Court" 1996). After the 2010 election, three justices with equal claims to the job agreed to share the duties over the next two years, with each serving eight months as chief justice Michael L. Douglas from January to September 2011, Nancy M. Saitta from September 2011 to May 2012, and Michael A. Cherry from May 2012 until January 2013 ("NV Supreme Court" 2012).

12. The norm was challenged in 2014, when Justice Costa M. Pleicones sought to unseat Chief Justice Jean H. Toal. Ultimately, Toal was reelected by a 95–74 vote of the General Assembly (Borden 2014). The Republican-dominated state legislature returned to the seniority custom when it elevated the "liberal-leaning" Pleicones in 2015 (Bantz 2015) and African American justice Donald W. Beatty by a unanimous vote in 2016. Beatty had served in the legislature as a Democrat during the 1990s. Notably, some conservative lawmakers attempted to recruit a challenger to Beatty in 2016 but were unsuccessful (Monk 2016).

13. Serranus C. Hastings also served as chief justice of two states. Hastings was the chief justice of Iowa from 1848 to 1849 and the first chief justice of California, from 1849 to 1851.

14. For more information about Beatty's judicial career, see his biographical sketch in *The National Cyclopaedia of American Biography* ("Beatty, William Henry" 1904).

15. It is apparent that Smith took the position's leadership of the judicial branch seriously, as he was an enthusiastic promoter of judicial reform and court unification as early as 1915 (S. Smith 1916). Interestingly, he also called for the chief justiceship to be elected statewide rather than determined by seniority in office (S. Smith 1916; Waller and Goza 2010).

16. Modern chief justices who served at least 20 years include Gerald W. Vande-Walle of North Dakota, Randall T. Shepard of Indiana, Robert C. Murphy of Maryland, Thomas J. Moyer of Ohio, Sharon Keller of Texas, and David E. Gilbertson of South Dakota.

17. Updated PAJID data (since 2007) come from Hughes and Wilhelm 2021.

18. Some differences exist between our methodologies. A minor difference is that Langer and Wilhelm refer to "rotation/seniority" systems as "random." A more substantive difference occurs in our classification of state systems. Specifically, we classified 19 states differently than Langer and Wilhelm did. We also account for changes over time within a state, while the analysis by Langer and Wilhelm does not. States with changes over time include Idaho, New York, Utah, Virginia, and Wisconsin.

Chapter 2

1. Using the larger data set of state supreme court judges assembled by Goclzhauser (2016), we omitted individuals who did not serve as chief justices, supplemented the original data set to fill omissions where possible, and altered data entries when necessary to reflect each individual's experience when becoming chief justice rather than when joining the high court.

2. One borderline case in our data was Buell A. Nesbett, the first chief justice of Alaska. Nesbett served briefly as a municipal magistrate and referee in bankruptcy court earlier in his career (Pace 1993), and contemporaneous newspaper accounts refer to him as a police judge. Those positions are more limited in jurisdiction and

powers than the prior positions of most judges in our data, but we consider Nesbett's positions sufficient to record him as having prior judicial experience.

3. For more information on Hubbell, see the biographical sketch by Dumas (2020). Krivosha has been characterized as "Governor Exon's political jack-of-all-trades" and "point man on political issues during virtually all of Exon's two gubernatorial terms" (Hewitt 2007, 84, 86). Despite joining the court with no prior judicial experience, Krivosha was eager to assert himself as the state's top judge, but he was unable to achieve most of his goals and was resented by his colleagues for his attempts to change their behavior and work environment (87–88).

4. For more information about Holt's tenure as chief justice, see Dumas 2018.

5. McKean had also served as president of the Continental Congress. After leaving the state supreme court, he was governor of Pennsylvania again, from 1799 to 1808.

6. "O'Connor Draws Record Turnout" 1986, 4.

7. Given the brief and intentionally temporary nature of Weltner's tenure as chief justice, he is omitted from our statistical analyses.

8. The six chief justices who previously served as governors were John Cromwell Bell Jr. of Pennsylvania, Ernest W. McFarland of Arizona, C. William O'Neill of Ohio, Richard J. Hughes of New Jersey, John W. King of New Hampshire, and G. Mennen Williams of Michigan. Bell served as governor for only 19 days, in January 1947.

9. See the career retrospective by Belknap (1987) for more information about the political and judicial roles of Chief Justice Hughes. For information about Hughes's advocacy activities in the 1970s, see Sullivan 1977.

10. "Injudicious: Supreme Court Objection to Reform is Unseemly," *Dallas Morning News*, February 11, 1987, 18A.

11. The earliest nonwhite and female justices were Jonathan Jasper Wright of South Carolina (African American) and Florence E. Allen of Ohio (female). Notably, three Jewish men led state high courts prior to the modern era (Henry A. Lyons of California, Franklin J. Moses Sr. of South Carolina, and Benjamin N. Cardozo of New York).

12. Two additional women, Judith W. Rogers and Annice M. Wagner, served as chief judges of the District of Columbia Court of Appeals in the 1980s and 1990s.

13. As of 2021, the states without a female chief justice in their high court history include Delaware, Hawaii, Nebraska, North Dakota, Pennsylvania, Rhode Island, South Dakota, Vermont, and Kentucky. The Texas Supreme Court has never had a female chief justice, but the Texas Court of Criminal Appeals has been led by Sharon Keller since 2001.

14. For a list of the state's chiefs since statehood, compiled by the New Mexico Courts, see "Chief Justices of the Supreme Court of the State of New Mexico" 2020.

15. For a biographical sketch of Dorothy Comstock Riley's mother, Josephine Grima, see Mellon 2019.

16. Goelzhauser's (2016) analysis also includes control variables for court professionalism and term length, which we chose not to include. Notably, the indicator most used for court professionalism (Squire 2008; see also Squire and Butcher 2021) does not vary over time for most of the years of our analysis. Consequently, we maintain that state fixed effects absorb any explanatory power that indicator might have. In addition, term length for a chief justice is difficult to standardize for courts with term lengths for "duration of service" or with the guideline of serving "till 70." This fluidity presents a measurement problem for inclusion of that variable. For that

reason and because no control variables in Goelzhauser's models reach statistical significance, we opted not to include those somewhat problematic variables.

17. See Chappell 1997 for biographical sketches of several African American chief justices who served during the mid-1990s, including Chief Justice Freeman.

Chapter 3

1. "Supreme Court Names Courthouse after Calogero," *Ouachita Citizen*, December 14, 2019.

2. Newby's full set of responses to the questionnaire is archived at Ballotpedia (see "Paul Martin Newby" 2021).

3. For thorough historical studies of judicial administration and court reform in the United States, see, for example, C. B. Graham 1993, Hays and Douglas 2006, Kasparek 2005, Raftery 2015, and Tobin 1999.

4. Our research did reveal instances where administrative leadership of the state judiciary was shared with associate justices. However, those unusual arrangements were circumstantial, temporary modifications. For example, Chief Justice Nix, chief justice in Pennsylvania and the first Black chief justice, was stripped of his administrative authority in 1989 due to a "quiet" revolt within the state supreme court. The revolt was related to a sensational and antagonistic relationship between Nix and Associate Justice Rolf Larsen, who was ultimately impeached for misbehavior in office (Lounsberry and Zausner 1996). Administrative leadership on the court ultimately fell to the justice who could get the necessary favorable votes, per the revised procedure. In 2021, the Colorado Supreme Court divided up administrative duties between all its members when allegations of misconduct were made against high-ranking judicial officials, including former Chief Justice Nathan B. "Ben" Coats. The newly appointed Chief Justice Brian D. Boatright identified that the safeguard and sharing of power would remain in place until the wrongdoing had been addressed (Bradbury 2021).

5. Conn. Gen. Stat. ch. 870, sec. 51-1b, available online at https://www.cga.ct .gov/current/pub/chap_870.htm#sec_51-1b

6. Ga. Const. art. VI, available online at https://law.justia.com/constitution/ge orgia/conart6.html

7. Ala. Code § 12-2-30 (1975).

8. Florida Rules of Judicial Administration, available online at https://www.fl courts.org/content/download/217909/file/Florida-Rules-of-Judicial-Administration .pdf

9. Data obtained from the National Center for State Courts (NCSC) and through our own web searches. A judicial council may also be known as a judicial conference or a board for judicial administration. States that have a judicial council that is not led by the chief include Arkansas, New Mexico, Oklahoma, Tennessee, and Wisconsin. States without a judicial council include Colorado, Connecticut, Florida, Montana, Rhode Island, Vermont, and West Virginia. In the remaining 38 states, the chief justice chairs the council.

10. In Alabama, this authority includes the ability to appoint temporary justices to the state supreme court.

11. To supplement data obtained from the National Center for State Courts, we collected data from websites of state courts and state administrative offices of courts. Specifically, from information available about 29 state supreme courts, we found that chief justices had authority to appoint temporary judges as needed in 24 states and to establish special committees in 26 states.

12. "About the Oregon Judicial Department," Oregon Judicial Branch, October 17, 2021. https://www.courts.oregon.gov/about/Pages/default.aspx

13. NCSC data reveal that 8 of the 29 surveyed court systems reported that their chief justices were authorized to appoint quasi-judicial officers.

14. These extrajudicial duties of court leaders were identified on the websites of the relevant ethics commissions: see Colorado Commission on Judicial Discipline 2021; Center for Judicial Ethics, n.d.; Commission on Judicial Conduct 2021.

15. See Miss. Const. art. XIII, § 254; Alas. Const. art. VI, § 8; Colo. Const. art. V, § 48; N.J. Const. art. IV, § 3, ¶ 2.

16. Miss. Const. art. XIII, § 254.

17. Chief Justice Reynoldson discussed the administrative role of Iowa's chief justice in an oral history interview archived by the Iowa Judicial Branch ("Honorable W. Ward Reynoldson" 2017).

18. "In Tribute: Chief Justice Howell T. Heflin," *Cumberland Law Review* 7, no. 3 (Winter 1977): 385–86.

19. "Tribute to Daniel L. Herrmann, Chief Administrator of Justice," *Delaware Journal of Corporate Law* 10, no. 2 (1985): 371.

20. Alexander Hamilton, "Federalist No. 78," in *The Federalist: The Famous Papers on the Principles of American Government*, ed. Benjamin F. Wright (New York: Barnes & Noble Books, 1996), 490.

Chapter 4

1. "Racial Justice Statements from the Courts (2020)," *Self-Represented Litigation Network*, October 21, 2021, https://www.srln.org/node/1442/race-justice-statements-courts-2020

2. Virginia Chief Justice Edward W. Hudgins offered remarks at meetings of the Virginia Judicial Conference from its establishment in 1950 until his death in 1958. Related documents are housed among his personal papers in the collection of the Library of Virginia.

3. Pringle remained a leading advocate for innovation in the judicial branch. During the 1970s, he served as president of the Conference of Chief Justices, helped establish and served as president of the National Center for State Courts, and chaired the board of directors of the American Judicature Society (Pringle 2014).

4. While 25 State of the Judiciary reports were analyzed by Rausch (1981), only 24 were delivered by the chief justice. Rausch reported that the Pennsylvania address was given to the state bar association by Justice Samuel J. Roberts because Chief Justice Henry X. O'Brien was ill.

5. The states where the first State of the Judiciary address we found was delivered to a state bar meeting were Alabama, Arizona, California, Florida, Georgia, Hawaii, Idaho, Illinois, Kansas, Maine, Massachusetts, Minnesota, Missouri, Nebraska, North Carolina, Ohio, Pennsylvania, South Carolina, Tennessee, Utah, Vermont, Washington, West Virginia, and Wyoming.

6. The states where the earliest State of the Judiciary message we identified was delivered orally to a state legislature were Alaska, Connecticut, Indiana, Iowa, Kentucky, Louisiana, Maryland, Michigan, Montana, New Hampshire, New Jersey, New York, North Dakota, Oklahoma, Rhode Island, and South Dakota.

7. Recktenwald's message on social media was reprinted as text in Hawaiian news outlets (e.g., "Chief Justice Recktenwald Delivers State of the Judiciary through

Social Media" 2013). For his February 2021 report, Recktenwald produced a video presentation for the Hawaii legislature (https://www.youtube.com/watch?v=pzKJHd D9q0w), featuring illustrative photographs and video clips of statements from state citizens.

8. In some instances, State of the Judiciary remarks become a lasting part of a chief justice's legacy. The State of the Judiciary addresses delivered by Randall Shepard of Indiana were noted as memorable and productive when he stepped down after 25 years as chief justice. Dickson (2012, 590) described Shepard's addresses as "remarkable," "uplifting," "masterful," and "consistently well received by legislators of both parties."

9. See Tex. Gov't Code tit. 2, ch. 21, sec. 4, available online at https://statutes.ca pitol.texas.gov/Docs/GV/htm/GV.21.htm#21.004

10. Maine House of Representatives, House Communication 430, January 3, 2018.

11. Communication from Michael L. Douglas, February 1, 2011, *Journal of the Assembly of the State of Nevada, Seventy-Sixth Session*, 19–20.

Chapter 5

1. See articles about Chief Justice Hecht's address published in Texas news sources such as the *Houston Chronicle* (Cobler 2019), the *Austin American-Statesman* (Lindell 2019), and the *Waco Tribune-Herald* (Platoff and McCullough 2019).

2. Varnum v. Brien, 763 N.W.2d 862.

3. In some states and years, chief justices focused on updates and general appeals, including zero requests for reform in their State of the Judiciary addresses. While such focus is not very common, it is not entirely rare.

4. Those items represent a subset of the 1,746 requests analyzed in chapter 4. Comparable data for the other variables in our multivariate analysis were not available for all years. We chose a time period, beginning in 1990, in which data were available for all variables of importance.

5. The Westlaw database can be found at www.Westlaw.com. Westlaw's database tracking state legislative activity can be searched by state and year. We identified substantive keywords for each proposal and searched for those terms in the bill-tracking database for each state/year. For example, a proposal that called for court interpreters would include the search terms *interpreter, judicial,* and *court.* Westlaw's search results include all bills that contain the relevant search terms in the bill text or related contents.

6. The National Center for State Courts maintains a database of legislative activity related to state courts since 2006, at its *Gavel to Gavel* blog (https://www.ncsc.org /gaveltogavel).

References

"About the Oregon Judicial Department." Oregon Judicial Branch, October 17, 2021. https://www.courts.oregon.gov/about/Pages/default.aspx

Acquaviva, Gregory L., and John D. Castiglione. "Judicial Diversity on State Supreme Courts." *Seton Hall Law Review* 39, no. 4 (2009): 1203–62.

Administrative Office of the U.S. Courts. "Table JCI—U.S. Federal Courts Federal Judicial Caseload Statistics (March 31, 2019)." Administrative Office of the U.S. Courts, 2019. https://www.uscourts.gov/statistics/table/jci/federal-judicial-casel oad-statistics/2019/03/31

Alabama Legislature. "Powers and Duties as to Supervision and Administration of Courts Generally." In *Code of Alabama 1975*, tit. 12, ch. 2, sec. 30. http://alisondb .legislature.state.al.us/alison/codeofalabama/1975/coatoc.htm

Alaska Legislature. "Redistricting Board." In *The Constitution of the State of Alaska*, art. 6, sec. 8 (amended 1998). https://ltgov.alaska.gov/information/alaskas-constit ution/

Alfini, James J., Shailey Gupta-Brietzke, and James F. McMartin IV. "Dealing with Judicial Misconduct in the States: Judicial Independence, Accountability and Reform." *South Texas Law Review* 48, no. 4 (Summer 2007): 889–910.

Allen, Peter. "California Chief Justice Speaks Out on Addressing Racism and Bias." California Courts Newsroom, June 8, 2020. https://newsroom.courts.ca.gov/ne ws/california-chief-justice-speaks-out-addressing-racism-and-bias

Alozie, Nicholas O. "Black Representation on State Judiciaries." *Social Science Quarterly* 69, no. 4 (December 1988): 979–86.

Alozie, Nicholas O. "Distribution of Women and Minority Judges: The Effects of Judicial Selection Methods." *Social Science Quarterly* 71, no. 2 (June 1990): 314–25.

Armstrong, Ken, and Rick Pearson. "Heiple Quits as Top Justice, Stays on Court." *Chicago Tribune*, May 3, 1997. https://www.chicagotribune.com/news/ct-xpm-19 97-05-03-9705030175-story.html

Ashley, Bob. "Chief Justice Post Eludes Pivarnik." *Post-Tribune*, February 14, 1987, A1.

Associated Press. "Busiest Circuit is N. Virginia." *Washington Post*, May 12, 1962, C3.

Associated Press. "Far-Right View Helps Moore in Alabama." *Journal-Gazette* (Fort Wayne, IN), September 28, 2017.

Associated Press. "Georgia Supreme Court Selects New Chief Justice." Associated Press, April 17, 2018.

Associated Press. "Indiana Supreme Court Functions Despite Rancor." *Post-Tribune*, October 30, 1989, B4.

Associated Press. "Michigan Chief Justice." *Grand Rapids Press*, November 27, 2001, C7.

Associated Press. "Police Say No Proof to Shepard Rumors." *Post-Tribune*, October 29, 1988, A8.

Bacon, C. Shannon. "State of the Judiciary." Speech presented in the Chamber of the New Mexico House of Representatives, Santa Fe, NM, January 24, 2023.

Bailey, Frank H., and Jag C. Uppal. "The State of the Judiciary." In *The Book of the States*, edited by the Council of State Governments, 87–101. Lexington, KY: Council of State Governments, 1976.

Bakst, M. Charles. "Jan. 1, 1935: 'The Bloodless Revolution': On That Day, Democratic Coup Changed State Government." *Providence Journal*, October 13, 1985, C1.

Bantz, Phillip. "SC Supreme Court Elections: A Change in the Lineup." *South Carolina Lawyers Weekly*, February 26, 2015.

Barnett, Helaine M. "Chief Judge Kaye's Legacy of Innovation and Access to Justice." *New York University Law Review* 92, no. 1 (April 2017): 6–10.

Barron, David J. "Making Policy Off the Bench: Putting the Role of State Court Leaders in Context." In *The Role of State Court Leaders in Supporting Public Policy That Affects the Administration of Justice: A Conference Report and Profiles of State Inter-Branch Initiatives*. Philadelphia: Pew Center on the States and National Center for State Courts, 2008.

Barrow, Deborah J., and Thomas G. Walker. *A Court Divided: The Fifth Circuit Court of Appeals and the Politics of Judicial Reform*. New Haven: Yale University Press, 1988.

Bauer, Scott. "Justice Cast Vote Making Her 'Chief': Emails Detail Contested Leadership Issue." *St. Paul Pioneer Press*, May 1, 2015, A4.

"Beatty, William Henry." In *The National Cyclopaedia of American Biography*, 12: 268. New York: James T. White, 1904.

Beck, Molly. "Shirley Abrahamson Drops Lawsuit to Regain Chief Justice Title." *Chippewa Herald*, November 10, 2015.

Belknap, Michal R. "Chief Justice Richard J. Hughes: Leadership and Liberal Activism." *Seton Hall Law Review* 17, no. 1 (1987): 4–41.

Bell, Clark. "Judicial History of the Supreme Court of the State of Wyoming." *Medico-Legal Journal* 26, no. 3 (1908–9): 177–82.

Berger, Steven A. "Chief Justice Slams Court Critics." *New Hampshire Union Leader*, January 23, 1998.

Bergstrom, Bill. "Chief Justice Urges Lawmakers to Spend More Money on Courts." *Tampa Bay Times*, February 12, 1993, 6B.

Berkson, Larry C. "The Emerging Ideal of Court Unification." *Judicature* 60, no. 8 (1977): 372–82.

Berry, William D., Richard C. Fording, Evan J. Ringquist, Russell L. Hanson, and Carl Klarner. "A New Measure of State Government Ideology, and Evidence That Both the New Measure and an Old Measure Are Valid." *State Politics and Policy Quarterly* 13, no. 2 (2013): 164–82.

Berry, William D., Evan J. Ringquist, Richard C. Fording, and Russell L. Hanson. "Measuring Citizen and Government Ideology in the American States, 1960–93." *American Journal of Political Science* 42 (1998): 327–48.

Betts, Jack. "Chief Justice Deserves Hearing on Courts' Needs." *Charlotte Observer*, March 30, 2003.

Billings, Warren M. "The Supreme Court of Louisiana and Its Chief Justices." *Law Library Journal* 89, no. 4 (Fall 1997): 449–62.

Bliven, Luther F. "Cuomo Prepares to Name Judge—the New Chief." *Post-Standard*, February 22, 1993, B5.

Bluestein, Greg. "Budget Cuts Clog Justice System." *Hawk Eye*, October 27, 2011, 8B.

Borchardt, Jackie. "Gov. Mike DeWine Signs Bill Creating Partisan Races for State's Top Court." *Cincinnati Enquirer*, July 1, 2021. https://www.cincinnati.com/story/news/politics/2021/07/01/ohio-gov-mike-dewine-signs-partisan-judicial-election-bill/7831532002/

Borden, Jeremy. "Toal Re-elected as Chief Justice." *Post and Courier*, February 6, 2014, 2.

Bowling, Cynthia J., and Margaret R. Ferguson. "Divided Government, Interest Representation, and Policy Differences: Competing Explanations of Gridlock in the Fifty States." *Journal of Politics* 63, no. 1 (2001): 182.

Brace, Paul, Laura Langer, and Melinda Gann Hall. "Measuring the Preferences of State Supreme Court Judges." *Journal of Politics* 62, no. 2 (2000): 387–413.

Bradbury, Shelly. "Chief Justice Admits 'Crisis of Confidence.'" *Denver Post*, February 19, 2021, 1A.

Brennan, William J. "State Constitutions and the Protections of Individual Rights." *Harvard Law Review* 90, no. 3 (1977): 489–504.

Brown, Melissa. "Alabama Chief Justice Candidate Tom Parker: 'I Know What We Need.'" *Montgomery Advertiser*, October 15, 2018. https://www.montgomeryadvertiser.com/story/news/politics/2018/10/15/alabama-chief-justice-race-tom-parker-reiterates-conservative-bonafides-race-against-bob-vance/1646293002/

Bryant, Bobby. "General Assembly Elects Gregory as Chief Justice." *The State* (Columbia, SC), January 21, 1988, 1A.

Bureau of Economic Analysis. "Regional Economic Accounts." Bureau of Economic Analysis, U.S. Department of Commerce, 2022. https://apps.bea.gov/regional/downloadzip.cfm

Burger, Warren E. "The State of the Judiciary, 1970." *American Bar Association Journal* 56, no. 10 (1970): 929–34.

Caher, John. "Judge Kaye Lifts a Page from Tabloid Coverage of Courts." *Albany Times Union*, April 4, 1997, B2.

Cannon, Mark W. "Innovation in the Administration of Justice, 1969–1981: An Overview." *Policy Studies Journal* 10, no. 4 (1982): 668–79.

Caruso, Vincent. "The Illinois Supreme Court Elected Anne Burke Chief Justice as Ald. Ed Burke Faces a 14-Count Indictment on Federal Corruption Charges." Illinois Policy, September 11, 2019. https://www.illinoispolicy.org/anne-burke-named-chief-justice-of-illinois-supreme-court-while-husband-faces-corruption-charges/

Cauthen, James N. G. "State Constitutional Policymaking in Criminal Justice Procedure: A Longitudinal Investigation." *Criminal Justice Policy Review* 10, no. 4 (1999): 521–45.

Census Bureau. "Historical Population Change Data (1910–2020)." United States

Census Bureau, 2021. https://www.census.gov/quickfacts/fact/table/US/PST0 45221

Center for Judicial Ethics. "Judicial Ethics Advisory Committees by State." National Center for State Courts, n.d. https://www.ncsc.org/__data/assets/pdf_file/0029 /17498/judicialethicsadvisorycommitteesbystate.pdf

Chandler, Kim. "Alabama Justice Denies Telling Judges to Block Gay Marriages." Associated Press, June 21, 2016.

Chandler, Kim. "Few Options for Roy Moore as Alabama Certifies Jones Win." Associated Press, December 29, 2017.

Chappell, Kevin. "Record Number of Black Chief Justices: Six Jurists Head D.C. and State Supreme Courts." *Ebony Magazine*, October 1997, 122–30.

Charnock, Carolyn Karr. "Lack of Interest Cancels State Judiciary Speech." *Charleston Daily Mail*, January 26, 1996, 6B.

Chernick, Richard. "The Stolz Report: Poor Marks for Rose Bird." *Los Angeles Lawyer* 5, no. 1 (March 1982): 8–10.

"Chief Justices of the Supreme Court of the State of New Mexico." New Mexico Courts, 2020. https://supremecourt.nmcourts.gov/wp-content/uploads/sites /3/2020/12/Chief-Justices-since-statehood1.pdf

"Chief Justice Recktenwald Delivers State of the Judiciary through Social Media." *Hawaii News Now*, February 7, 2013. https://www.hawaiinewsnow.com/story/210 09962/chief-justice-delivers-state-of-judiciary-through-social-media/

Christie, Andrew D., and Nancy C. Maron. "Find a Better Way to Work with the Legislature." *Judges' Journal* 30, no. 3 (Summer 1991): 15–17, 42–43.

Claremont School District v. Governor of New Hampshire. 142 N.H. 462, 465, 703 A.2d 1353, 1354 (1997).

Clark, Tom. "A Note on the Moore Cases and Judicial Administration." *Justice System Journal* 26, no. 3 (2005): 355–61.

Cobler, Paul. "Chief Justice Urges Nonpartisan Posts." *Houston Chronicle*, February 7, 2019, A4.

Collins, Ronald K. L., and Peter J. Galie. "Models of Post-Incorporation Judicial Review: 1985 Survey of State Constitutional Individual Rights Decisions." *Publius: The Journal of Federalism*, 16 no. 3 (Summer 1986): 111–40.

Colorado Commission on Judicial Discipline. "About Us." October 17, 2021. http:// www.coloradojudicialdiscipline.com/About_us.html

Colorado General Assembly. "Revision and Alteration of Districts—Reapportionment Commission." In *The Constitution of the State of Colorado*, Art 5, Sec. 48 (amended November 4, 1974). https://www.sos.state.co.us/pubs/info_center/laws/COCo nstitution/ColoradoConstitution.pdf

Commission on Judicial Conduct. "Judicial Ethics Advisory Committee Overview." Arizona Supreme Court, 2021. https://www.azcourts.gov/azcjc/JudicialEthicsAd visoryCommittee/Overview.aspx

Connecticut General Assembly. "Chief Justice of the Supreme Court, Duties and Powers." In *The General Statutes of Connecticut*, ch. 870, sec. 51-1b. https://www.cga.ct .gov/current/pub/chap_870.htm#sec_51-1b

Council of State Governments. "Book of the States." Council of State Governments, 2020. https://web.archive.org/web/20200822205818/http://knowledgecenter .csg.org/kc/category/content-type/content-type/book-states

Council of State Governments. *The Book of the States*. Lexington, KY: Council of State Governments, 2021.

Court Statistics Project. "CSP Annual Caseload Reports." National Center for State Courts and Conference of State Court Administrators, 2020. https://www.cour tstatistics.org

Cross, Frank B., and Stefanie Lindquist. "The Decisional Significance of the Chief Justice." *University of Pennsylvania Law Review* 154, no. 6 (2006): 1665–1707.

Dake, Lauren. "Lawmakers Grow Weary of Talk by Chief Justice." *Columbian,* January 5, 2015, C1.

Danelski, David J. "The Influence of the Chief Justice in the Decisional Process of the Supreme Court." Paper presented at the Annual Meeting of the American Political Science Association, New York, September 8–10, 1960.

Danelski, David J., and Artemus Ward, eds. *The Chief Justice: Appointment and Influence.* Ann Arbor: University of Michigan Press, 2016.

Dickson, Brent E. "A Tribute to Randall T. Shepard—Justice, Indiana Supreme Court, 1985–2012; Chief Justice of Indiana, 1987–2012." *Indiana Law Review* 45, no. 3 (2012): 585–92.

DiFiore, Janet M. "The State of Our Judiciary 2020." Speech presented at Court of Appeals Hall, Albany, NY, February 26, 2020. https://www.nycourts.gov/ctapps /news/20_SOJ-Speech.pdf

Dixon, Ken. "Republicans Say No to McDonald as Court Chief." *Darien News-Review,* March 30, 2018, A12.

Dosal, Sue K., Mary C. McQueen, and Russell R. Wheeler. "'Administration of Justice Is Archaic': The Rise of the Modern Court Administration; Assessing Roscoe Pound's Court Administration Prescriptions." *Indiana Law Journal* 82, no. 5 (2007): 1293–1305.

Douglas, James W., and Roger E. Hartley. "The Politics of Court Budgeting in the States: Is Judicial Independence Threatened by the Budgetary Process?" *Public Administration Review* 63, no. 4 (July–August 2003): 441–54.

Douglas, James W., and Roger E. Hartley. "State Court Budgeting and Judicial Independence: Clues from Oklahoma and Virginia." *Administration and Society* 33, no. 1 (March 2001): 54–78.

Douglas, Michael. Communication from Michael L. Douglas. February 1, 2011. *Journal of the Assembly of the State of Nevada, Seventy-Sixth Session,* 19–20. https://www.leg .state.nv.us/Session/76th2011/Journal/Assembly/Final/aj001.pdf

Dubois, Phillip L., ed. *The Politics of Judicial Reform.* Lexington, MA: Lexington Press, 1982.

Dubois, Phillip L., and Keith O. Boyum. "Court Reform: The Politics of Institutional Change." In *Handbook of Court Administration and Management,* edited by Steven W. Hays and Cole Blease Graham Jr., 27–51. New York: Marcel Dekker, 1993.

Ducat, Craig R., and Victor E. Flango. *Leadership in State Supreme Courts: Roles of the Chief Justice.* Beverly Hills, CA: SAGE, 1976.

Dumas, Earnest. "Jack Wilson Holt Jr. (1929–)." *Encyclopedia of Arkansas,* October 25, 2018. https://encyclopediaofarkansas.net/entries/jack-wilson-holt-jr-7548/

Dumas, Earnest. "Webster Lee (Webb) Hubbell (1948–)." *Encyclopedia of Arkansas,* November 17, 2020. https://encyclopediaofarkansas.net/entries/webster-lee-we bb-hubbell-1948-8694/

Dura, Jack. "North Dakota Supreme Court Justice Jon Jensen is Next Chief Justice." *Bismarck Tribune,* December 13, 2019.

Egelko, Bob. "Bird Goes, Cranston Stays: Grodin, Reynoso Also Lose." *Daily Breeze,* November 5, 1986, A1.

Egelko, Bob. "The Lucas Years, 1987–1996." In *Constitutional Governance and Judicial Power: The History of the California Supreme Court*, edited by Harry N. Scheiber, 515–61. Berkeley: Berkeley Public Policy Press, 2016.

Egelko, Bob. "The State Supreme Court: Right, Left and Center." *Daily Journal*, September 2, 2006. https://dailyjournal.com/articles/312072-the-state-supreme-court-right-left-and-center

Elbow, Steven. "Crime and Courts: GOP Looks to End Liberal Lock on Chief Justice Job." *Capital Times*, July 7, 2011.

Emmert, Craig F., and Carol Ann Traut. "State Supreme Courts, State Constitutions, and Judicial Policymaking." *Judicial System Journal* 16, no. 1 (1992): 37–48.

Eshbaugh-Soha, Matthew. "The Importance of Policy Scope to Presidential Success in Congress." *Presidential Studies Quarterly* 40, no. 4 (2010): 708–24.

Estreicher, Samuel, and Oscar G. Chase. "Chief Judge Judith S. Kaye: A Modern-Day Arthur Vanderbilt." *New York University Law Review* 84, no. 3 (June 2009): 651–52.

Ewald, Michael. "Chief Justice Gilbertson: More than a Legacy." *The South Dakotan Lawyer*, March 9, 2022. https://www.usd.edu/academics/colleges-and-schools/knudson-school-of-law/south-dakotan-lawyer/chief-justice-gilbertson-more-than-a-legacy

Fife, Madelyn, Greg Goelzhauser, and Stephen T. Loertscher. "Selecting Chief Justices by Peer Vote." *State Politics and Policy Quarterly* 21, no. 2 (2021): 165–94.

Fish, Peter G. *The Politics of Federal Judicial Administration*. Princeton: Princeton University Press, 1973.

Flango, Carol R., Deborah W. Smith, Charles F. Campbell, Elizabeth Maddox, and Neal B. Kauder. *Trends in State Courts, 2015*. Williamsburg, VA: National Center for State Courts, 2015.

Florida Rules of Judicial Administration. January 24, 2018. https://www.flcourts.org/content/download/217909/file/Florida-Rules-of-Judicial-Administration.pdf

Florida Supreme Court. "Canady Re-elected as Chief Justice of the Florida Supreme Court." Press release, Craig Waters, Florida Supreme Court, October 28, 2019. https://www.floridasupremecourt.org/content/download/539986/file/10-28-2019_Canady_Elected.pdf

Florida Supreme Court. "Carlos Muñiz Elected Chief Justice of the Florida Supreme Court." Press release, Paul Flemming, Florida Supreme Court, March 9, 2022. https://www.floridasupremecourt.org/content/download/831793/file/Muniz-Chief-Justice-03092022.pdf

Friesen, Ernest. "Constraints and Conflicts in Court Administration." In *Managing the State Courts*, edited by Larry C. Berkson, Steven W. Hays, and Susan J. Carbon, 38–44. St. Paul, MN: West, 1977.

Gallas, Geoff. "Court Reform: Has It Been Built on an Adequate Foundation?" *Judicature* 63, no. 1 (1979): 28–38.

Garrett, Robert T. "What Texas Lawmakers May Sacrifice to Get Judges a Pay Raise." *Dallas Morning News*, May 14, 2019. https://www.dallasnews.com/news/politics/2019/05/14/what-texas-lawmakers-may-sacrifice-to-get-judges-a-pay-raise/

Gavel to Gavel (blog). National Center for State Courts. https://www.ncsc.org/gaveltogavel

Gavin, Robert. "Vote Raises Questions about Court Transparency." *Times Union* (Albany, NY), September 19, 2022, A1, A5.

Gazell, James A. "Five Great Issues in Judicial Administration." In *Handbook of Public Administration*, 3rd ed., edited by Jack Rabin, W. Bartley Hildreth, and Gerald J. Miller, 1029–59. New York: Taylor and Francis, 2006.

Georgia General Assembly. "Judicial Branch." In *The Constitution of the State of Georgia*, art. 6 (1983). https://law.justia.com/constitution/georgia/conart6.html

Gertner, Nancy. "To Speak or Not to Speak: Musings on Judicial Silence." *Hofstra Law Review* 32, no. 4 (2004): 1147–62.

Glick, Henry R. *Courts, Politics, and Justice*. New York: McGraw-Hill, 1983.

Glick, Henry R. "Innovation in State Judicial Administration: Effect on Court Management and Organization." *American Politics Quarterly* 9, no. 1 (1981): 49–69.

Glick, Henry R. "Policy-Making and State Supreme Courts: The Judiciary as an Interest Group." *Law and Society Review* 5, no. 2 (1970): 271–92.

Glick, Henry R. "The Politics of Court Reform: In a Nutshell." *Policy Studies Journal* 10, no. 4 (1982): 680–89.

Goelzhauser, Greg. "Diversifying State Supreme Courts." *Law and Society Review* 45, no. 3 (2011): 761–81.

Goelzhauser, Greg. *Choosing State Supreme Court Justices: Merit Selection and the Consequences of Institutional Reform*. Philadelphia: Temple University Press, 2016.

Gold, David M. *The Shaping of Nineteenth-Century Law: John Appleton and Responsible Individualism*. Westport: Greenwood Press, 1990.

Gouras, Matt. "Chief Justice Tries to Pre-empt Legislative Proposal." Associated Press, January 31, 2003.

Graham, Barbara Luck. "Do Judicial Selection Systems Matter? A Study of Black Representation on State Courts." *American Politics Quarterly* 18, no. 3 (1990): 316–36.

Graham, Cole Blease, Jr. "Reshaping the Courts: Traditions, Management Theories, and Political Realities." In *Handbook of Court Administration and Management*, edited by Steven W. Hays and Cole Blease Graham Jr., 3–25. New York: Marcel Dekker, 1993.

Grass, James. "Healing the Rift between Indiana Supreme Court Members Will Be Difficult Now That Justice Alfred Pivarnik Has Charged That Chief Justice Randall T. Shepard Abused Alcohol and Drugs before Being Named to the High Court." *USA Today*, October 28, 1988.

Gray, Thomas, and Banks Miller. "Swineherds and Hogs on Ice: Leadership Impacts for State Chief Judges." *American Politics Research* 49, no. 3 (2021): 319–27.

Greene, Lisa. "High Court Candidates Facing Tall Issues." *The State* (Columbia, SC), May 6, 1994, A1.

Grubb, Ignatius C. "The Supreme Court of Delaware." *Medico-Legal Journal* 12, no. 3 (1894): 351–64.

Hackett, George W. "Gabbard Fighting Stephens for Judgeship." *Lexington (KY) Herald-Leader*, October 21, 1984, B1.

Hager, Philip. "Drug Cases Imperil Courts." *Los Angeles Times*, February 13, 1990, 1.

Hager, Philip. "Lucas Details Plan for Studying Drug Crisis Legal System: The Chief Justice's State of the Judiciary Talk Focuses on Long-Term Efforts to Understand Problems Facing the Courts." *Los Angeles Times*, March 5, 1991, 3.

Hager, Philip. "President of Judges Unit Raps Bar Assn. Judiciary: He Says the Lawyers Failed to Fight Legislative Moves to Slash the Supreme Court's Budget, Allowing Themselves to Be Muzzled by Politicians." *Los Angeles Times*, October 5, 1992, 3.

Hall, Dee J. "Lawmakers Mull Proposal to Allow Justices to Select Chief State Supreme Court." *Wisconsin State Journal*, November 3, 2013, A1.

Hall, Matthew E. K., and Jason H. Windett. "Discouraging Dissent: The Chief Judge's Influence in State Supreme Courts." *American Politics Research* 44, no. 4 (2016): 682–709.

Hall, Melinda Gann. "Opinion Assignment Procedures and Conference Practices in State Supreme Courts." *Judicature* 73, no. 4 (1990): 209–14.

Hamilton, Alexander. "Federalist No. 78." In *The Federalist: The Famous Papers on the Principles of American Government*, edited by Benjamin F. Wright, 489–96. New York: Barnes and Noble Books, 1996.

Hannah, Jim. "State of the Judiciary." Speech presented at the Hot Springs Convention Center, Hot Springs, AR, June 11, 2011.

Hartley, Roger E. "It's Called Lunch: Judicial Ethics and the Political and Legal Space for the Judiciary to Lobby." *Arizona Law Review* 56, no. 2 (2014): 383–410.

Hartley, Roger E., and James W. Douglas. "Budgeting for State Courts: The Perceptions of Key Officials Regarding the Determinants of Budget Success." *Justice System Journal* 24, no. 3 (2003): 251–63.

Hayes, Anna R. *Without Precedent: The Life of Susie Marshall Sharp*. Chapel Hill: University of North Carolina Press, 2008.

Haynie, Stacia L. "Leadership and Consensus on the U.S. Supreme Court." *Journal of Politics* 54, no. 4 (1992).

Hays, Steven W. "Staffing the Bench: Personnel Management and the Judiciary." In *Handbook of Court Administration and Management*, edited by Steven W. Hays and Cole Blease Graham Jr., 221–36. New York: Marcel Dekker, 1993.

Hays, Steven W., and James W. Douglas. "Judicial Administration: Modernizing the Third Branch." In *Handbook of Public Administration*, 3rd ed., edited by Jack Rabin, W. Bartley Hildreth, and Gerald J. Miller, 983–1028. New York: Taylor and Francis. 2006.

Hecht, Nathan L. "The State of the Judiciary in Texas." Speech presented in the Chamber of the Texas House of Representatives, Austin, TX, February 6, 2019.

Herrmann, Daniel L. "State of the Judiciary Address." Speech presented at the Ninth Annual Delaware Joint Bench-Bar Conference, Wilmington Country Club, Wilmington, Delaware, June 5, 1974.

Hewitt, James W. *Slipping Backward: A History of the Nebraska Supreme Court*. Lincoln: University of Nebraska Press, 2007.

Holewa, Sally. "Court Reform: The North Dakota Experience." *Justice System Journal* 30, no. 1 (2009): 91–110.

Holman, Rhonda. "Eagle Editorial: Snub of Chief Justice Was Rude." *Wichita Eagle*, January 4, 2013.

Holman, Rhonda. "Process for Picking Justices Works Well." *Wichita Eagle*, February 3, 2016.

"Honorable W. Ward Reynoldson." Iowa Judicial Branch, August 17, 2017. https://www.iowacourts.gov/for-the-public/educational-resources-and-services/iowa-courts-history/oral-interviews-with-past-judges/honorable-w-ward-reynoldson/

Hood, W. B. "Rose Bird's Opponents Gear Up for TV Blitz." *Los Angeles Times*, September 20, 1978, A1.

Horsey, Henry R., and William Duffy. "The Supreme Court after 1951: The Separate Supreme Court." Delaware Courts, 1993. https://courts.delaware.gov/supreme/history/history3.aspx

Hughes, David A., Richard L. Vining Jr., and Teena Wilhelm. "The Politics of the U.S. Federal Judiciary's Requests for Institutional Reform." *Social Science Quarterly* 98, no. 5 (2017): 1277–95.

Hughes, David A., and Teena Wilhelm. "Measuring the Preferences of State Supreme Court Justices: A PAJID Update." Unpublished manuscript, November 2021, typescript.

Hughes, David A., Teena Wilhelm, and Richard L. Vining Jr. "Deliberation Rules and Opinion Assignment Procedures in State Supreme Courts: A Replication." *Justice System Journal* 36, no. 3 (2015): 395–410.

Hurwitz, Mark S., and Drew Noble Lanier. "Diversity in State and Federal Appellate Courts: Change and Continuity across 20 Years." *Justice System Journal* 29, no. 1 (2008): 47–70.

Hurwitz, Mark S., and Drew Noble Lanier. "Explaining Judicial Diversity: The Differential Ability of Women and Minorities to Attain Seats on State Supreme and Appellate Courts." *State Politics and Policy Quarterly* 3, no. 4 (2003): 329–52.

"Injudicious: Supreme Court Objection to Reform Is Unseemly." *Dallas Morning News*, February 11, 1987, 18A.

"In Tribute: Chief Justice Howell T. Heflin." *Cumberland Law Review* 7, no. 3 (Winter 1977): 381–92.

Jacobs, Paul. "California Elections / Proposition 140 Initiative Cuts More Than Terms of Office." *Los Angeles Times*, October 28, 1990, 3.

Jefferson, Wallace. "Reform from Within: Positive Solutions for Elected Judiciaries." *Seattle University Law Review* 33, no. 3 (Spring 2010): 625–32.

Jonsson, Patrik. "Roy Moore: The Alabama Judge Who 'Relishes' Gay Marriage Fight." *Christian Science Monitor*, January 7, 2016.

Kabler, Phil. "Author of Book on W.Va. Corruption also Fined $10K." *Charleston Gazette-Mail*, February 14, 2019, 1A.

Kagan, Robert A., Bliss Cartwright, Lawrence M. Friedman, and Stanton Wheeler. "The Evolution of State Supreme Courts." *Michigan Law Review* 76 (1978): 961–1005.

Karlik, Michael. "Q&A with Mary Mullarkey: First Female, Longest-Serving Supreme Court Chief Justice." *Colorado Politics*, July 2, 2021. https://www.coloradopolitics.com/q-and-a/q-a-with-mary-mullarkey-first-female-longest-serving-supreme-court-chief-justice/article_394d416c-81bc-11eb-89fb-3b52b7e3125c.html

Karmeier, Lloyd A. Opening Remarks at Budget Appropriation Hearings. Illinois Senate Appropriation Hearings, April 18–19, 2018.

Karnig, Albert K., and Lee Sigelman. "State Legislative Reform and Public Policy: Another look." *Western Political Quarterly* 28, no. 3 (1975): 548–52.

Kasler, Karen. "The State of Ohio." Ideastream Public Media, July 10, 2020. https://www.ideastream.org/programs/state-of-ohio/covid-19-red-zone-masks-a-must-voting-preps-begin-chief-justice-in-studio?_ga=2.106377411.1914662130.1614449240-208975096.1614449240

Kasparek, F. Dale, Jr. "Leading the Unfinished Reform: The Future of Third Branch Administration." Project report submitted for Phase III of the Court Executive Development Program, Institute for Court Management, 2005. https://www.ncsc.org/__data/assets/pdf_file/0022/16474/kasparekdaleccdpfinal.pdf

Katches, Mark. "Wilson Pick for Next Chief Justice Cited." *Daily News of Los Angeles*, March 16, 1996, N1.

Kavanagh, Thomas M. "The State of the Judiciary." *Michigan State Bar Journal* 50, no. 4 (April 1971): 196–204.

Kaye, Judith S. "My Transition to Chief Judge." In *Judith S. Kaye: In Her Own Words*, edited by Henry M. Greenberg, Luisa M. Kaye, Marilyn Marcus, and Albert M. Rosenblatt, 53–60. Albany: State University of New York Press, 2019.

Kaye, Judith S. "Women Chiefs: Shaping the Third Branch." *University of Toledo Law Review* 36, no. 4 (Summer 2005): 899–904.

Kendall, John A. "President's Message, Proposing an Inventory of Ourselves and Our Profession." *Res Gestae* 14, no. 2 (February 1971), 5–6, 22–23, 29.

Kennedy, John. "Labarga to Remain as Chief Justice Role." *Palm Beach Post*, February 6, 2016, 1B.

Kenney, Sally J. "Choosing Judges: A Bumpy Road to Women's Equality and a Long Way to Go." *Michigan State Law Review* 5 (2012): 1499–1528.

Kincaid, John. "State Constitutions in the Federal System." *Annals of the American Academy of Political and Social Science* 496, no. 1 (1988): 12–22.

King, John W. "Justice King: 'State of the Judiciary.'" *New Hampshire Law Weekly* 9, no. 40 (1983): 435–37.

Klein, Fannie J., and Ruth J. Witztum. "Judicial Administration, 1972–1973." *Annual Survey of American Law* 1972, no. 4 (Summer 1973): 717–48.

Kleps, Ralph N. "Tribute to Chief Justice Donald R. Wright." *Hastings Constitutional Law Quarterly* 4, no. 4 (Fall 1977): 683–87.

Koplowitz, Howard. "Doug Jones to Be Sworn into Senate Seat Wednesday on Family Bible." *Birmingham News*, December 31, 2017. https://www.al.com/news/2017/12/doug_jones_to_be_sworn_into_se.html

Kowalick, Claire. "Texas Bill Boosts Pay for Judges, Prosecutors." *Abeline Reporter-News*, August 26, 2019, A4.

Kritzer, Herbert M. *Judicial Selection in the States: Politics and the Struggle for Reform.* New York: Cambridge University Press, 2020.

Krueger, Joline Gutierrez. "In Pursuit of Justice." *Albuquerque Tribune*, February 12, 2003, A1.

Langer, Laura, Jody McMullen, Nicolas P. Ray, and Daniel D. Stratton. "Recruitment of Chief Justices on State Supreme Courts: A Choice between Institutional and Personal Goals." *Journal of Politics* 65, no. 3 (2003): 656–75.

Langer, Laura, and Teena Wilhelm. "The Ideology of State Supreme Court Chief Justices." *Judicature* 89, no. 2 (2005): 78–86.

Leach, Jeff. "Governor Abbott Signs Three Measures Authored by Representative Leach." June 19, 2019. https://house.texas.gov/news/press-releases/?id=7006

Legislature v. Eu. 54 Cal. 3d 492 (1991).

Leonard, Meghan E., and Joseph V. Ross. "Gender Diversity, Women's Leadership, and Consensus in State Supreme Courts." *Journal of Women, Politics, and Policy* 41, no. 3 (2020): 278–302.

Lindell, Chuck. "Texas Chief Justice Calls for Bail Reform." *Austin American-Statesman*, web edition, February 6, 2019. https://www.statesman.com/story/news/politics/state/2019/02/06/texas-chief-justice-calls-for-bail-reform-end-to-partisan-election-of-judges/6076816007/

Linhares, Gregory J. "Vision, Function, and the Kitchen Sink: The Evolving Role of the State Court Administrator." In *Future Trends in State Courts*, edited by Carol R. Flango, Amy M. McDowell, Deborah W. Saunders, Nora E. Sydow, Charles F. Campbell, and Neal B. Kauder, 20–25. Williamsburg, VA: National Center for State Courts, 2012.

Lippman, Jonathan. "Chief Judge S. Kaye: A Visionary Third Branch Leader." *New York University Law Review* 84, no. 3 (June 2009): 655–61.

Lobato v. Taylor. 71 P.3d 983 (2002).

Lounsberry, Emilie, and Robert Zausner. "Nix to Step Down from High Court: The Son of a Politically Powerful Family Headed the Court in a Rough Time; He'll Leave by the End of the Year." *Philadelphia Inquirer*, March 7, 1996, A1.

Lupton, John A. "Choosing the Chief." *Bench & Bar* 53, no. 2 (2022): 1–3.

Magnuson, Eric. "Electing Justice: Minimize Politics in Judge Selection." *Minnesota Lawyer*, October 12, 2020.

Magnuson, Eric. "Reflections on My (Brief) Time as Chief Justice." *Hennepin Lawyer* 78, no. 1 (2008): B1.

Maine House of Representatives. House Communication 430. January 3, 2018. *Journal and Legislative Record, House of Representatives, One Hundred and Twenty-Eighth Legislature, State of Maine*, H-1279. Maine State Law and Legislative Reference Library. http://lldc.mainelegislature.org/Open/LegRec/128/House/LegRec_2018-02-08_HD_pH1278-1282.pdf

Marcin, Phillip J. "Deciding the Deciders: The Diffusion of State Supreme Court Selection Procedures." PhD diss., University of Georgia, 2015.

Marcin, Phillip J., and Nancy Marion. "Agenda Setting in State Courts of Last Resort." *Journal of Criminal Justice and Law* 3, no. 1 (2019): 37–57.

Marley, Patrick. "Supreme Court Justices Will Choose Their Chief; Voters Back Change to State Constitution." *Milwaukee Journal Sentinel*, April 8, 2015, 10.

Martin, Douglas. "John Hill, 83, Is Dead; Texas Democrat Who Served in Many Positions." *New York Times*, July 16, 2007.

Martin, Elaine, and Barry Pyle. "Gender and Racial Diversification of State Supreme Courts." *Women and Politics* 24, no. 2 (2002): 35.

Mason, Alpheus T. "The Burger Court in Historical Perspective." *Political Science Quarterly* 89, no. 1 (1974): 27–45.

Mayhew, David. *Congress: The Electoral Connection.* New Haven: Yale University Press, 1974.

McConnell, Edward B. "The Administrative Office of the Courts of New Jersey." *Rutgers Law Review* 14, no. 2 (1960): 290–303.

McConkie, Stanford S. "Decision-Making in State Supreme Courts: A Look Inside the Conference Room." *Judicature* 59, no. 7 (1976): 337–43.

McConkie, Stanford S. "Environmental, Institutional, and Procedural Influence in Collegial Decision-Making: A Comparative Analysis of State Supreme Courts." PhD diss., Michigan State University, 1974.

McKee, Jennifer. "Bill Targeting Probation Officers Bashed." *Independent Record*, February 20, 2003.

McKoski, Raymond J. "Interbranch Communication and Rule 3.2 of the 2007 ABA Model Code of Judicial Conduct." *Court Review* 50, no. 3 (2014): 150–57.

Medina, Harold R. "Judges as Leaders in Improving the Administration of Justice." *Journal of the American Judicature Society* 36, no. 1 (1952): 6–12.

Mellon, Mary. "Josephine Grima: IU's First Mexican Student." *Blogging Hoosier History*, January 29, 2019. https://blogs.libraries.indiana.edu/iubarchives/2019/01/29/josephine-grima/

Meschke, Herbert L., and Ted Smith. "The North Dakota Supreme Court: A Century of Advances." *North Dakota Law Review* 76, no. 2 (2000): 217–310.

Milstein, Susan. "Death Threat Ignored / Bird Speaks at Bar Convention." *San Francisco Chronicle*, September 15, 1986, 9.

Mintz, Howard. "Governor's Judicial Choices Defy Labels: Schwarzenegger's Picks Show Greater Diversity Than Those of GOP Predecessors." *San Jose Mercury News*, July 25, 2010, 1A.

Mississippi Legislature. "Senatorial and Representative Districts." In *The Constitution of the State of Mississippi*, art. 15, sec. 254 (amended November 2020). https://www.sos.ms.gov/content/documents/ed_pubs/pubs/Mississippi_Constitution.pdf

Moakley, Maureen, and Elmer E. Cornwell. *Rhode Island Politics and Government.* Lincoln: University of Nebraska Press, 2001.

Moline, Brian. "Justice William A. Johnston—the Grand Old Man of Kansas." *Journal of the Kansas Bar Association* 56, no. 4 (1987): 19–24.

Monk, John. "Beatty Picked to Lead South Carolina Supreme Court." *Anderson Independent-Mail,* web edition, May 26, 2016.

Moore, Russell J. "Frank Williams: Rhode Island's Enigma." Politics, GoLocalProv, April 15, 2015. https://www.golocalprov.com/politics/frank-williams-rhode-islands-enigma

Mosk, Stanley. "Phil Gibson—a Remembrance." *California Law Review* 72, no. 4 (July 1984): 506–9.

Mouat, Lucia. "Chief Judge of New York Resigns His Post Amid Scandal." *Christian Science Monitor,* November 12, 1992, 8.

Murphy, Walter F. *Elements of Judicial Strategy.* Chicago: University of Chicago Press, 1964.

Nelson, Jim. "Jean Turnage—one of a Vanishing Breed." *Independent Record,* October 7, 2015.

Nemacheck, Christine L. "The Path to Obergefell: Saying 'I Do' to New Judicial Federalism." *Washington University Journal of Law and Policy* 54 (2017): 149–68.

New Jersey Legislature. "Judicial." In *The Constitution of the State of New Jersey,* art. IV (amended November 2020). https://www.njleg.state.nj.us/constitution

Norris, Mikel. "Beyond Consensus: Gender, Chief Justices, and Leadership on State Supreme Courts." *Journal of Women, Politics, and Policy* 43, no. 2 (2022): 134–51.

Norris, Mikel, and Holley Tankersley. "Women Rule: Gendered Leadership and State Supreme Court Chief Justice Selection." *Journal of Women, Politics, and Policy* 39, no. 1 (2018): 104–25.

Norris, Mikel, and Charlie Hollis Whittington. "A Matter of Style: Perceptions of Chief Justice Leadership on State Supreme Courts with an Eye Toward Gendered Differences." *Judicature* 102, no. 2 (2018): 48–57.

"NV Supreme Court Gets New Leader." *Sparks Tribune,* May 8, 2012.

Obergefell v. Hodges. 576 U.S. 644 (2015).

"O'Connor Draws Record Turnout at Convention." *Montana Lawyer,* 1986, 3–4.

Pace, Eric. "Chief Justice Buell A. Nesbett, 83; Headed Alaska's Supreme Court." *New York Times,* August 23, 1993, D8.

"Paul Martin Newby." *Ballotpedia,* 2021. https://ballotpedia.org/Paul_Martin_Newby

Peck, John. "Chief Justice Worked Tirelessly." *Huntsville Times,* July 1, 2011, 11A.

Perry, H. W., Jr. *Deciding to Decide: Agenda Setting in the United States Supreme Court.* Cambridge, MA: Harvard University Press, 1991.

Pierson, Lacie. "Federal Jury Acquits Him of 10 Counts." *Charleston Gazette-Mail,* October 13, 2018, 1A.

Pitkin, Hanna F. *The Concept of Representation.* Berkeley: University of California Press, 1967.

Platoff, Emma, and Jolie McCullough. "Chief Calls for Judges to Run without Party Labels: Texas Supreme Court Chief Justice Nathan Hecht Calls for Nonpartisan Judicial Elections, Bail Reform." *Waco Tribune-Herald,* February 7, 2019, 1A.

Polsby, Nelson W. "The Institutionalization of the U.S. House of Representatives." *American Political Science Review* 62, no. 1 (1968): 144–68.

Poulos, John W. "The Judicial Philosophy of Roger Traynor." *Hastings Law Journal* 46, no. 6 (August 1995): 1643–1722.

Pound, Roscoe. "The Causes of Popular Dissatisfaction with the Administration of Justice." *American Lawyer* 14, no. 10 (October 1906): 445–51.

Pound, Roscoe. *Organization of Courts*. Boston: Little, Brown, 1940.

Pringle, Bruce D. "Four of the Greatest: Outstanding Lawyers in Colorado History." *Colorado Lawyer* 43, no. 7 (July 2014): 32–56.

"Proceedings of the Twenty-Third Annual Meeting of the Louisiana Bar Association." *Report of the Louisiana Bar Association* 21 (1920): 7–229.

"Racial Justice Statements from the Courts (2020)." Self-Represented Litigation Network, October 21, 2021. https://www.srln.org/node/1442/race-justice-statements-courts-2020

Raftery, William. "Chief Justices as Leaders: Roles and Challenges." In *The Book of the States, 2017*, edited by the Council of State Governments, 253–56. Lexington, KY: Council of State Governments, 2017.

Raftery, William. "Efficiency of Unified vs. Non-unified State Judiciaries: An Examination of Court Organizational Performance." PhD diss., Virginia Commonwealth University, 2015.

Raftery, William. "Unification and 'Bragency': A Century of Court Organization and Reorganization." *Judicature* 96, no. 6 (2013): 337–46.

Rausch, Amy K. "The State of the Judiciary: An Agenda for Change." *State Court Journal* 5, no. 1 (Winter 1981): 23–25, 41–43.

Reardon, Paul. "Chief Justice Burger and the National Center for State Courts." *Supreme Court Historical Society Yearbook*, 1986, 11–13.

Recktenwald, Mark E. "2021 State of the Judiciary." Speech presented at Aliʻiōlani Hale, Honolulu, Hawaii, February 5, 2021. YouTube video, 28:30. https://www.youtube.com/watch?v=pzKJHdD9q0w

Redman, Shane. "Diversity and Judicial Legitimacy in State Courts." PhD diss., University of Pittsburgh, 2021.

Reid, John. "Chief Justice Doe and Chief Justice Vanderbilt: A Comparison in the Techniques of Reform." *American Bar Association Journal* 46, no. 3 (1960): 278–328.

Roberts, Sam. "Ernest Finney Jr., Rights Lawyer in Pathbreaking Civil Rights Case, Dies at 86." *New York Times*, December 7, 2017, D6.

Robertson, Gary D. "Beasley Concedes Defeat in Chief Justice Race; Newby Elected." *Laurinburg Exchange*, December 14, 2020.

Roeder, Phillip W. "State Legislative Reform: Determinants and Policy Consequences." *American Politics Quarterly* 7, no. 1 (1979): 51.

Rogers, Josh, and Rick Ganley. "What to Expect from a N.H. Supreme Court Led by Gordon MacDonald." New Hampshire Public Radio, March 4, 2021. https://www.nhpr.org/nh-news/2021-03-04/what-to-expect-from-a-n-h-supreme-court-led-by-gordon-macdonald

Rosenthal, Cindy Simon. *When Women Lead: Integrative Leadership in State Legislatures*. New York: Oxford University Press, 1998.

Rottman, David B., and Shauna M. Strickland. *State Court Organization, 2004*. U.S. Department of Justice, Bureau of Justice Statistics, Washington, DC: Government Printing Office, 2006.

Rush, Loretta H. "2020 Indiana State of the Judiciary." Speech presented at the Indiana Statehouse, Indianapolis, January 15, 2020. https://www.in.gov/courts/supreme/state-of-judiciary/2020/

Saufley, Leigh I. Address to the Maine House of Representatives, February 16, 2017. *Journal and Legislative Record, House of Representatives, One Hundred and Twenty-*

158 · References

Eighth Legislature, State of Maine, H-139–43. Maine State Law and Legislative Reference Library. http://lldc.mainelegislature.org/Open/LegRec/128/House/Leg Rec_2017-02-16_HD_pH0133-0145.pdf

Scheiber, Harry N. "The Liberal Court: Ascendency and Crisis, 1964–1987." In *Constitutional Governance and Judicial Power: The History of the California Supreme Court,* edited by Harry N. Scheiber, 327–513. Berkeley: Berkeley Public Policy Press, 2016.

Scheiber, Harry N. "Special Section: Nine Speeches by Justice Roger J. Traynor." *California Legal History* 8 (2013): 211–74.

Scherer, Nancy, and Brett Curry. "Does Descriptive Race Representation Enhance Institutional Legitimacy? The Case of the U.S. Courts." *Journal of Politics* 72, no. 1 (2010): 90–104.

Sears, Leah Ward. "First Person: Leah Ward Sears, Chief Justice of the Georgia Supreme Court." *Atlanta Journal-Constitution,* June 21, 2009, E1.

Sears, Leah Ward. "2007 State of the Judiciary Address." Speech presented in the House Chambers, State Capitol, Atlanta, Georgia, January 24, 2007.

Selby, W. Gardner. "Great Jingle but No Top Spot for Hill." *Austin American Statesman,* July 12, 2007, B1.

Sentell, Will. "Chief Star Talks to General Assembly." *Kansas City Star,* January 15, 1992, C2.

Shaw, Dan. "Wisconsin Chief Justice Cites 'Bully Pulpit' as Source of Constitutional Amendment." *Wisconsin Law Journal,* November 6, 2013.

"Shearing to Lead Court." *Las Vegas Sun,* June 27, 1996.

Shepard, Randall T. "The Changing Nature of Judicial Leadership." *Indiana Law Review* 42, no. 4 (2009a): 767–72.

Shepard, Randall T. "Judith Kaye as a Chief among Chiefs." *New York University Law Review* 84, no. 3 (June 2009b): 671–75.

Sherman, Norville. "Obstacles to Implementing Court Reform." In *Managing the State Courts,* edited by Larry C. Berkson, Steven W. Hays, and Susan J. Carbon, 64–71. St. Paul, MN: West, 1977.

Slayton, David. Statement of David Slayton, Administrative Director, Office of Court Administration, Texas Judicial Council. *Hearings on H.B. 2384, Before the House Judiciary and Civil Jurisprudence Committee,* 86th Legislative Session (2019).

Smets, Kaat, and Carlien van Ham. "The Embarrassment of Riches? A Meta-analysis of Individual-Level Research on Voter Turnout." *Electoral Studies* 32, no. 2 (2013): 344–59.

Smith, Brad. "'State of Judiciary' Address Defends Court." *Golden Transcript* 105, no. 35, February 8, 1971. https://www.coloradohistoricnewspapers.org/?a=d&d=G OT19710208-01.2.7&srpos=8&dliv=none&e=——en-20-1–img-txIN%7ctxCO%7c txTA

Smith, Christopher E., and Heidi Feldman. "Burdens of the Bench: State Supreme Courts' Non-judicial Tasks." *Judicature* 84, no. 6 (2001): 304–9.

Smith, Sydney. "A Plea for the Establishment in Mississippi of a Modern Unified Court." *American Bar Association Journal* 2, no. 1 (1916): 27–45.

Southwick, Leslie. "Mississippi Supreme Court Elections: A Historical Perspective, 1916–1996." *Mississippi College Law Review* 18, no. 1 (Fall 1997): 115–98.

Squire, Peverill. "Measuring State Legislative Professionalism: The Squire Index Revisited." *State Politics and Policy Quarterly* 7, no. 2 (2007): 211–27.

Squire, Peverill. "Measuring the Professionalization of U.S. State Courts of Last Resort." *State Politics and Policy Quarterly* 8, no. 3 (2008): 223–38.

Squire, Peverill, and Jordan Butcher. "An Update to the Squire State Court of Last Resort Professionalization Index." *State Politics and Policy Quarterly* 21, no. 3 (2021): 326–33.

State of Louisiana v. Mitchell Smith. 99-KA-0606 (2000) (Calogero Jr., P. F., dissenting).

Stein, Robert A. "Causes of Popular Dissatisfaction with the Administration of Justice in the Twenty-First Century." *Hamline Law Review* 30, no. 3 (2007): 499–512.

Stephenson v. Bartlett. 562 S.E.2d 377 (N.C. 2002).

Stockmeyer, Norman Otto, Jr. "Hail to the Chiefs: A Tribute to America's Women Chief Justices." *Women Lawyers Journal* 80, no. 4 (September 1994): 9–18.

Stout, David. "Robert Wilentz, 69, New Jersey Chief Justice, Dies; Court Aided Women and the Poor." *New York Times*, July 24, 1996, D20.

Strebel, Erika. "Federal Judge Dismisses Abrahamson Lawsuit." *Wisconsin Law Journal*, July 31, 2015.

Sullivan, Joseph F. "Chief Justice Hughes Asks Raise of $12,500 for Judges in the State." *New York Times*, November 22, 1977, 79.

Sullum, Jacob. "How Roy Moore Failed to Reassure Voters He Is Not a Sexual Predator." *Reason*, December 13, 2017.

Sununu, Chris. "Sununu: 'I am Absolutely Disappointed' in MacDonald Vote." *New Hampshire Business Review*, July 11, 2019.

"Supreme Court Names Courthouse after Calogero." *Ouachita Citizen*, December 14, 2019. https://www.hannapub.com/ouachitacitizen/news/local_state_headlines /supreme-court-names-courthouse-after-calogero/article_d9f5fba8-21ab-11ea-b5 aa-e75cc78a35d6.html

"Supreme Court Rules Adopted by the Supreme Court of Nevada." Amended September 29, 2021. https://www.leg.state.nv.us/courtrules/scr.html

Sweet, Robin. "The Nevada Judiciary" In *Political History of Nevada*, 12th ed., edited by Barbara K. Cegavske, 241–84. Carson City: Nevada Secretary of State, 2016.

Swindler, William F. "Fifty-One Chief Justices." *Kentucky Law Journal* 60, no. 4 (1972): 851–71.

Tarr, G. Alan. "New Judicial Federalism in Perspective." *Notre Dame Law Review* 72, no. 4 (1997): 1097–1118.

Tarr, G. Alan. *Without Fear or Favor.* Palo Alto: Stanford University Press, 2012.

Taylor, Jessica. "The Crazy, Unbelievable Alabama Senate Race Careens to an End." *NPR*, December 11, 2017. https://www.npr.org/2017/12/11/569668106/the-cr azy-unbelievable-alabama-senate-race-careens-to-an-end

Terry, Charles L. "The Legislative Duty." *West Virginia State Bar News* 11, no. 25 (April 1964): 221–22.

Texas Legislature. "State of Judiciary Message." *Texas Government Code*, tit. 2, subtit. A, ch. 21, sec. 004 (2021). https://statutes.capitol.texas.gov/Docs/GV/htm/GV .21.htm#21.004

Timmons-Goodson, Patricia. "An Interview with Chief Justice Leah Ward Sears (Ret.)." *Judges' Journal* 49, no. 4 (2010): 4–6, 28.

Tobin, Robert W. *Creating the Judicial Branch: The Unfinished Reform.* Williamsburg, VA: National Center for State Courts, 1999.

Tobin, Robert W., and Richard B. Hoffman. 1979. *The Administrative Role of Chief Justices and Supreme Courts.* Washington, DC: National Center for State Courts, 1979.

"Tribute to Daniel L. Herrmann, Chief Administrator of Justice." *Delaware Journal of Corporate Law* 10, no. 2 (1985): 367–404.

Tucker, Katheryn Hayes. "Georgia's New High Court Leaders to Be Installed Today." *Fulton County Daily Report* 132, no. 126 (2021): 1.

Turner, Robert C., and Beau Breslin. "An Integrated Model of State Chief Justices' Governance Agenda." Unpublished manuscript, 2006, typescript.

United Press International. "Personality Spotlight; Joseph A. Bevilacqua: Rhode Island Chief Justice." May 28, 1986.

Uppal, Jag C. "The State of the Judiciary." In *The Book of the States*, edited by the Council of State Governments, 79–103. Lexington, KY: Council of State Governments, 1978.

Vanderbilt, Arthur T. *Minimum Standards of Judicial Administration.* New York: Law Center of New York University, 1949.

Varnum v. Brien. 763 N.W.2d 862 (2009).

Vining, Richard L., Jr., and Teena Wilhelm. "The Chief Justice as Advocate-in-Chief: Examining the Year-End Report on the Federal Judiciary." *Judicature* 95, no. 6 (2012): 267–74.

Vining, Richard L., Jr., Teena Wilhelm, and David A. Hughes. "The Chief Justice as Effective Administrative Leader: The Impact of Policy Scope and Interbranch Relations." *Social Science Quarterly* 100, no. 4 (2019): 1358–68.

Vining, Richard L., Jr., Teena Wilhelm, and Emily Wanless. "Succession, Opportunism, and Rebellion on State Supreme Courts: Decision to Run for Chief Justice." *Justice System Journal* 40, no. 4 (2019): 286–301.

Virginia State Bar. "Chief Justice Eggleston will Preside at Annual Meeting of the Judicial Conference on May 11 at Cavalier Hotel." *Virginia Bar News* 10, no. 4 (1962): 3.

Volsky, Igor. "Iowa Chief Justice Defends Marriage Decision, Judiciary Review: 'Courts Serve the Law.'" ThinkProgress, January 12, 2011. https://archive.thinkprogress .org/iowa-chief-justice-defends-marriage-decision-judiciary-review-courts-serve -the-law-632a81165000/

Wade, Christian. "MacDonald Joins New Hampshire Supreme Court Bench as New Chief Justice." Center Square, New Hampshire, January 25, 2021.

Walker, Thomas G., Lee Epstein, and William J. Dixon. "On the Mysterious Demise of Consensual Norms in the United States Supreme Court." *Journal of Politics* 50, no. 2 (1988): 361–89.

Waller, William L., Jr., and Gabe Goza. "The Office of Chief Justice of the Supreme Court of Mississippi." *Mississippi College Law Review* 29, no. 3 (2010): 469–98.

Wannamaker, George Noell. "Charles Longstreet Weltner: A Public Life." PhD diss., Georgia State University, 1999.

Warner, Sam Bass. "The Role of Courts and Judicial Councils in Procedural Reform." *University of Pennsylvania Law Review* 85, no. 5 (March 1937): 441–55.

Wathen, Daniel E. "When the Court Speaks: Effective Communication as Part of Judging." *Maine Law Review* 57, no. 2 (2005): 449–62.

Weideman, Paul. "Our Lovely Supreme Court Building." *Santa Fe New Mexican*, January 3, 2016.

Weltner, Charles L. "Justice Charles L. Weltner's Judicial Epitaph." *Journal of Southern Legal History* 3 (1994): 215–19.

White, Kate. "Rule Change Extends Loughry's Term as State's Chief Justice to Four Years." *Charleston Gazette-Mail*, April 7, 2017, 3C.

Wilhelm, Teena, Richard L. Vining Jr., Ethan D. Boldt, and Bryan M. Black. "Judicial Reform in the American States: The Chief Justice as Political Advocate." *State Politics and Policy Quarterly* 20, no. 2 (2020): 135–56.

Wilhelm, Teena, Richard L. Vining Jr., Ethan D. Boldt, and Allison Trochesset. "Examining State of the Judiciary Addresses: A Research Note." *Justice System Journal* 40, no. 2 (2019): 158–69.

Willoughby, William F. *Principles of Judicial Administration.* Washington, DC: Brookings Institution, 1929.

Winters, Glenn R. "The National Movement to Improve the Administration of Justice." *Journal of the American Judicature Society* 48, no. 1 (1964): 17–22.

Woelper, Willard G. "The Reorganization of the Judiciary in New Jersey." *Sydney Law Review* (1953): 46–63.

Zschirnt, Simon. "Gay Rights, the New Judicial Federalism, and State Supreme Courts: Disentangling the Effects of Ideology and Judicial Independence." *Justice System Journal* 37, no. 4 (2016): 348–66.

Index

Abbott, Greg W., 113
Abrahamson, Shirley S., 23, 49–50, 81
Access to justice, 13, 70, 120
Accountability courts, 13, 83, 98, 101–5, 110
Achieving judicial reform, 115–17
Administrative leader, chief justice, 2, 15, 39, 50, 67–71, 81–86, 129, 132, 135–36, 138, 141
Administrative powers, 2, 41, 66–67, 72
Administrative Office of the Courts, 87
Administrative reform, 50
Administrative reports, 87
Administrative responsibilities, 7, 9, 67–73, 81–83, 110, 114, 130
Administrator, chief justice as, 65–66, 70, 78, 87, 142
Adult probation system, 131
Advertising, by legislators, 115
Advocacy, chief justice, 9, 10, 39, 78, 81–83, 85–86, 92, 97, 111, 113–14, 123, 129, 133–34, 136, 140
Advocacy, public, 39, 81
African American, chief justices, 37, 46, 51–52, 54–55, 138–41
Agenda, judicial reform, 8, 75–77, 82, 85–86, 97, 110, 113–15, 117, 118, 120–22, 133–34

Agenda, legislative, 72, 81
Agenda, policy, 69, 111, 122
Agenda setting, 10, 76, 82–83, 86, 92, 97, 103, 105, 110, 119–20, 122, 126, 128–30, 134
Alabama, 1–2, 20–22, 32, 38, 41–43, 71, 78, 137, 141–42
Alabama Supreme Court, 1, 21
Alaska, 73, 97, 139–40, 142
Allen, Florence E., 140
Allen, Frederic W., 41, 43
Almand, Bond, 91
Alternative dispute resolution, 13
American Bar Association, 68–69, 76, 88
American Bar Association Standards Relating to Court Organization, 69
American Judicature Society, 68, 76, 100, 142
Anderson, John C., 28
Annual Report of the Administrative Director of the Courts of New Jersey (1948–49), 87–88
Apolitical, courts as, 115, 117, 130, 135
Appleton, John, 27, 29
Appointment, chief justice selection by, 18, 27, 32–34, 40, 42–44, 57–58, 60, 128, 138
Appointment powers, chief justice, 73

163